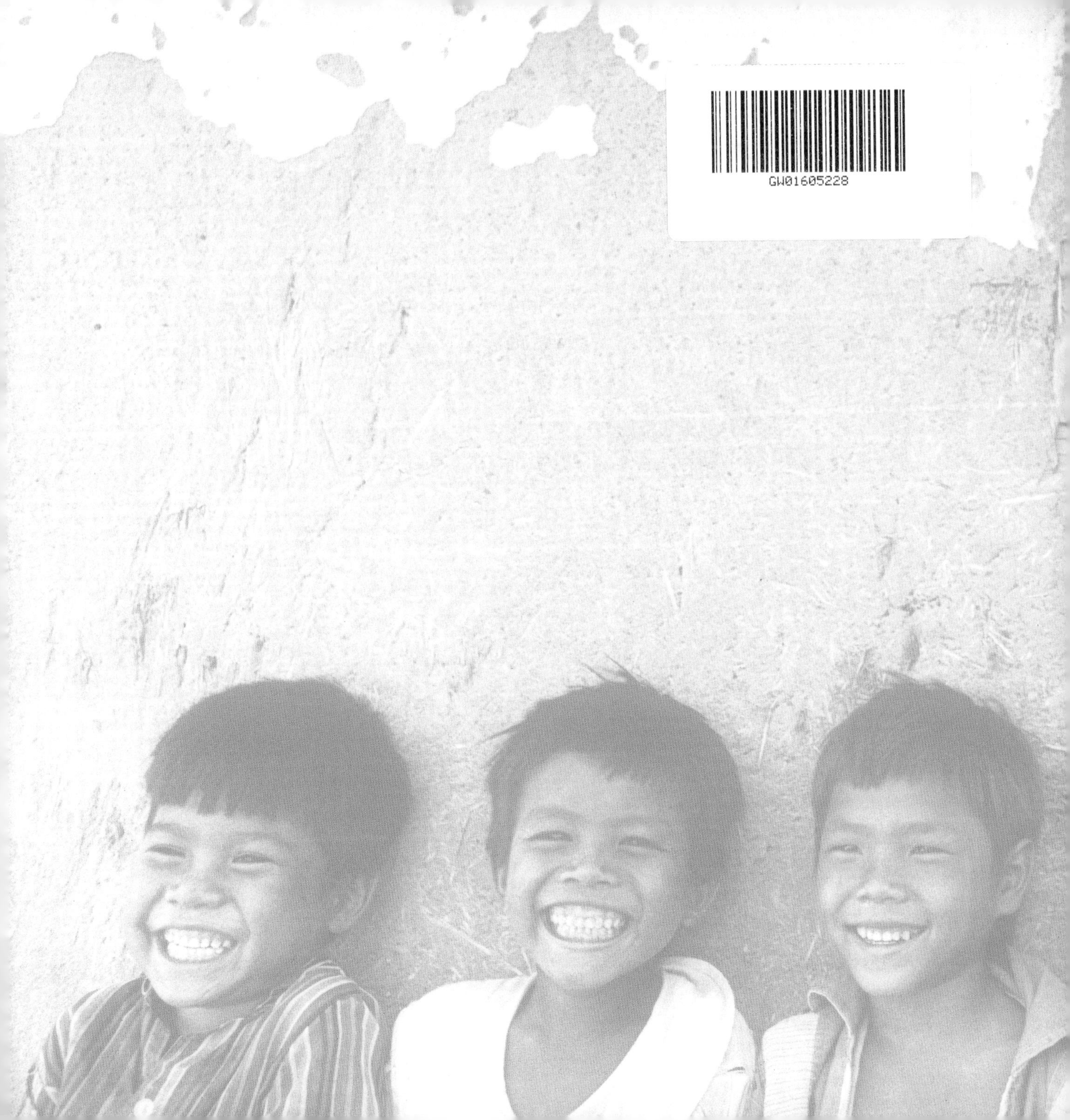
GW01605228

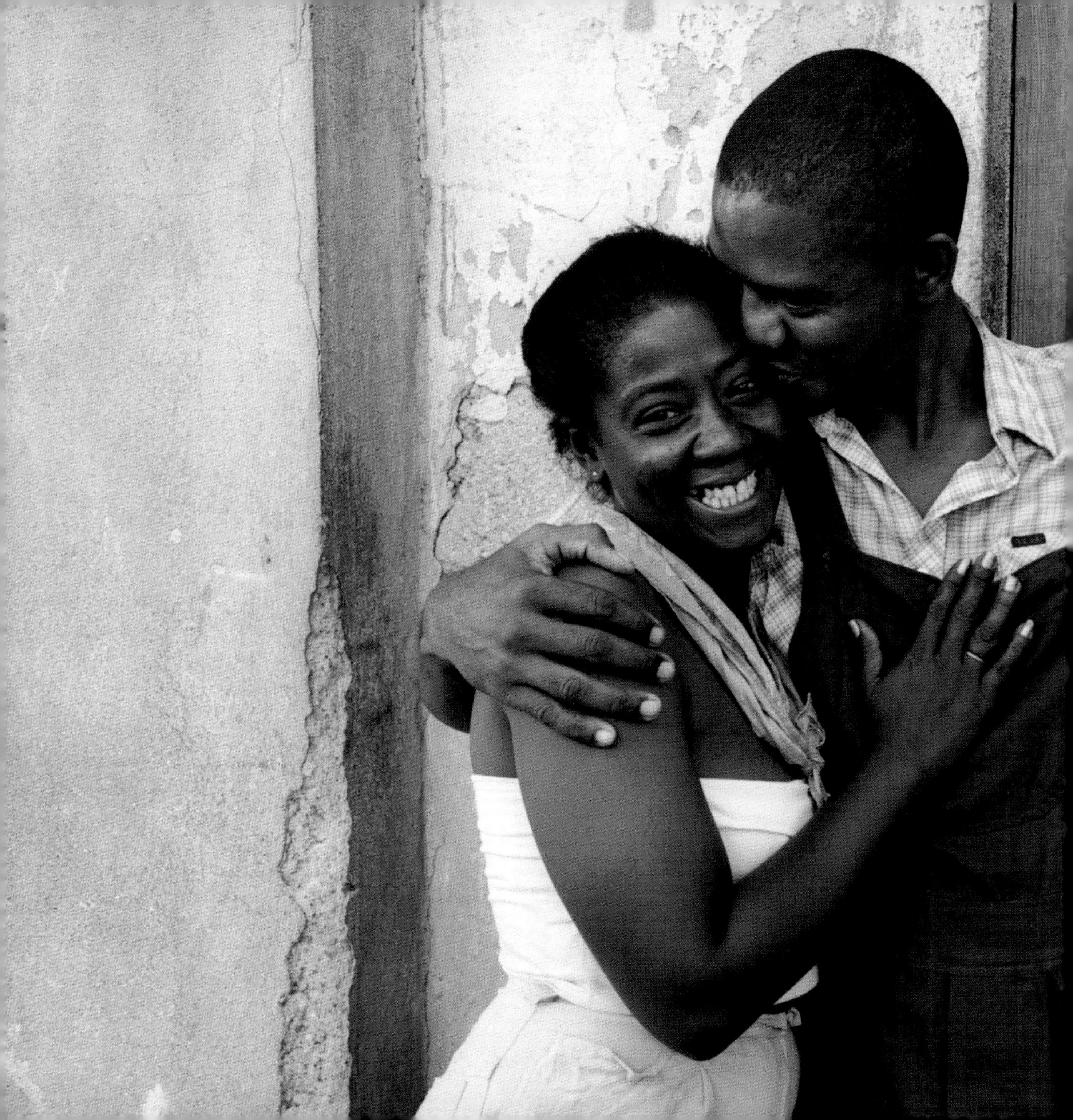

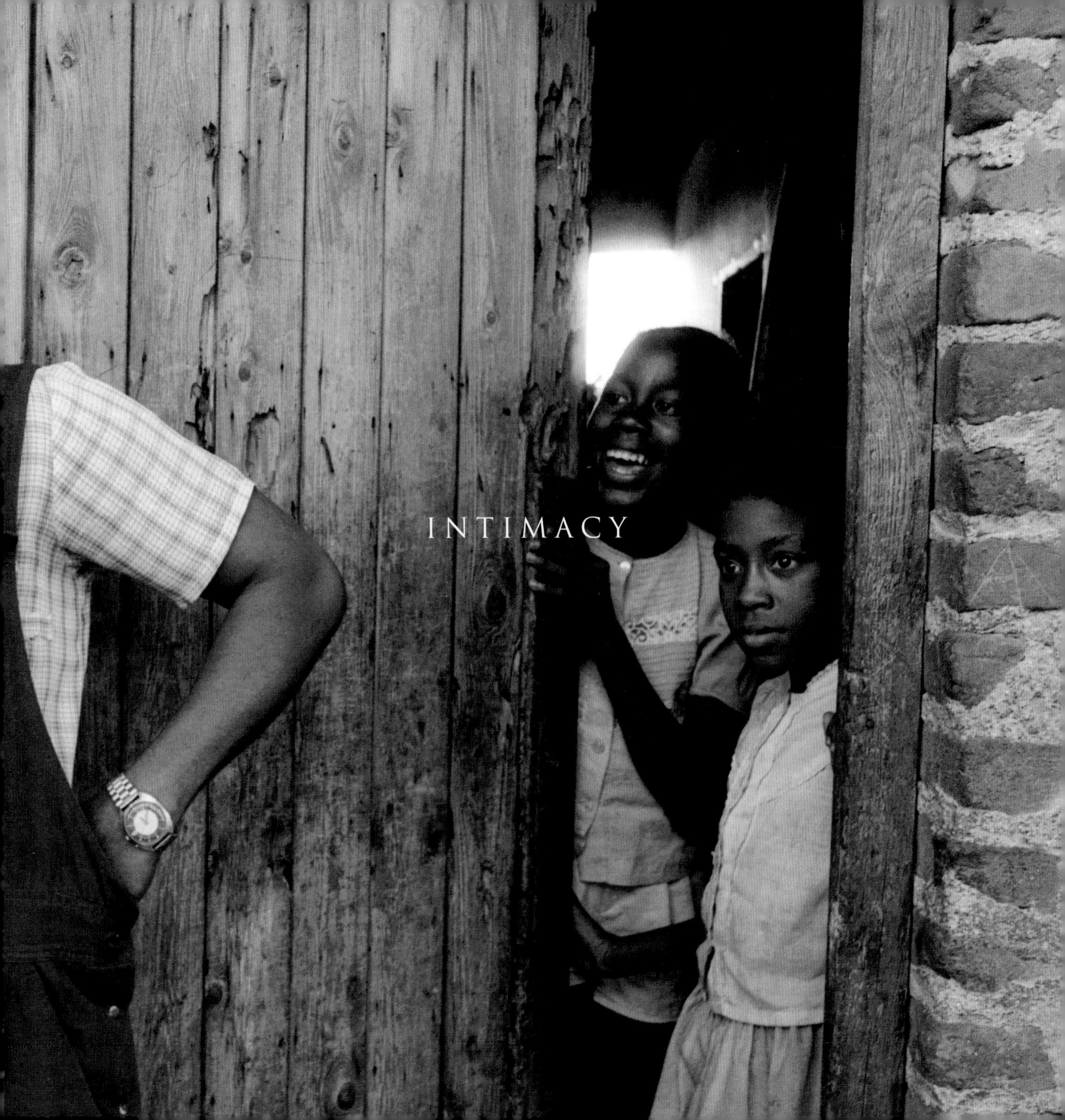

INTIMACY

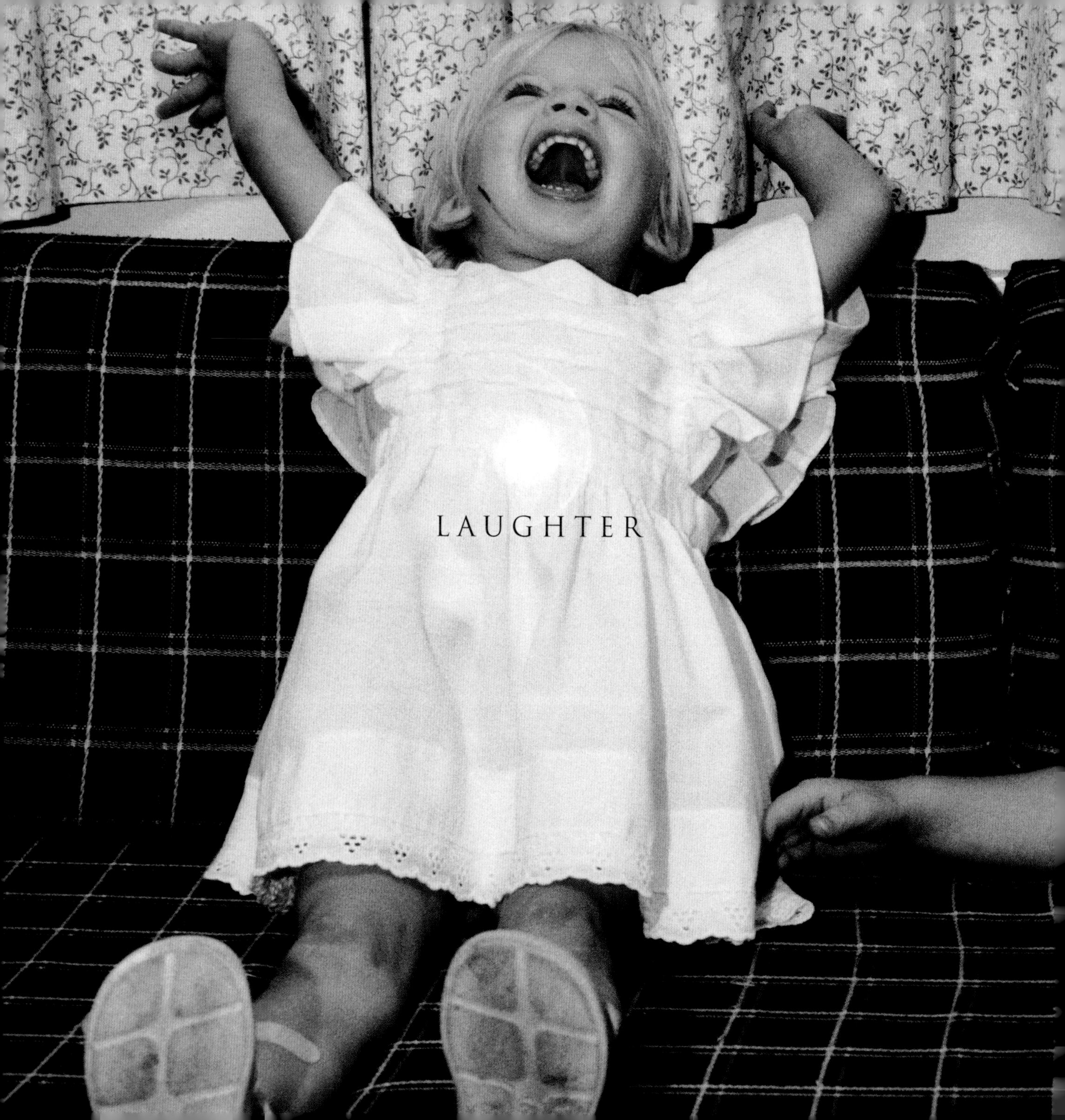

LAUGHTER

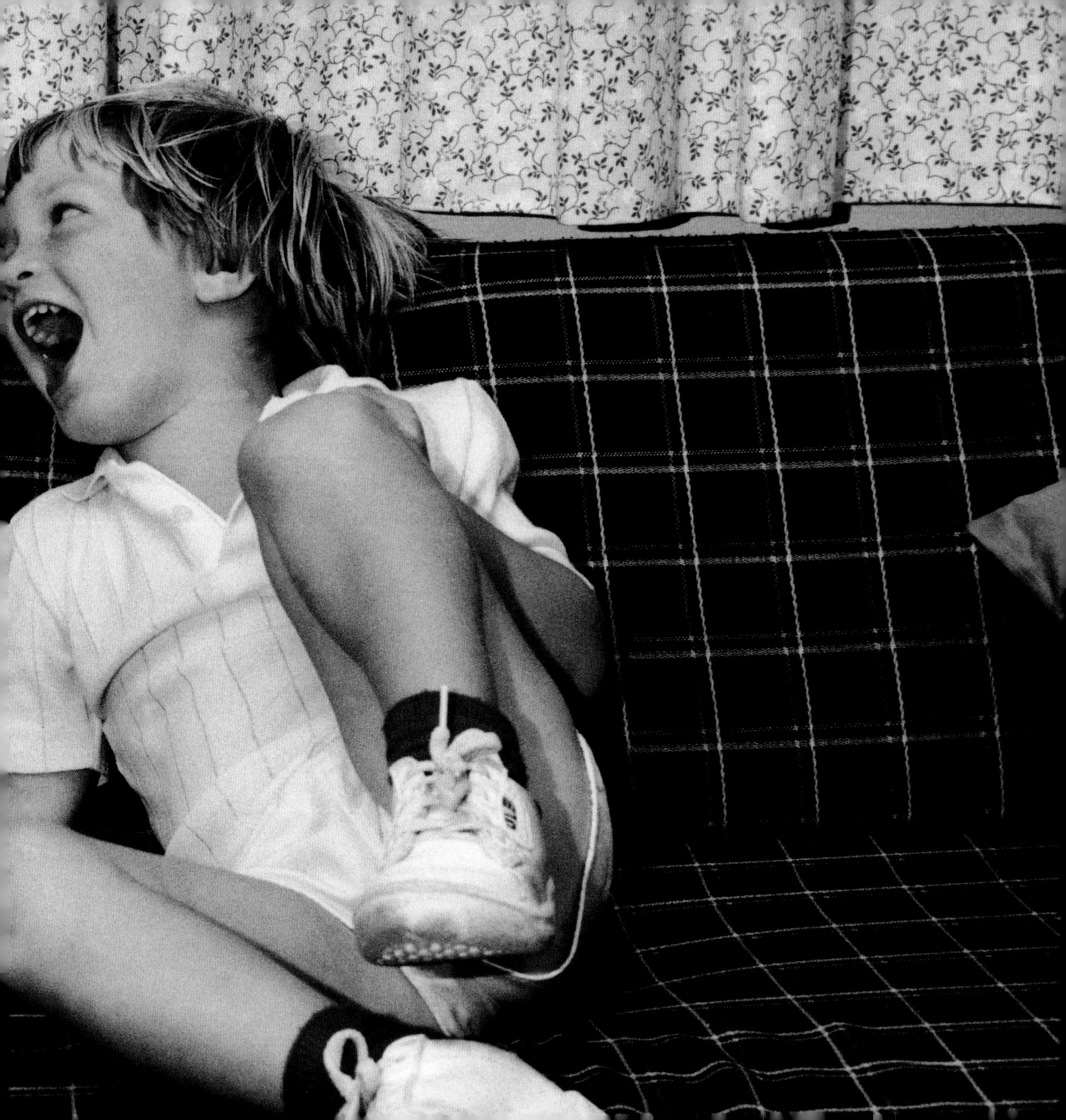

KINSHIP

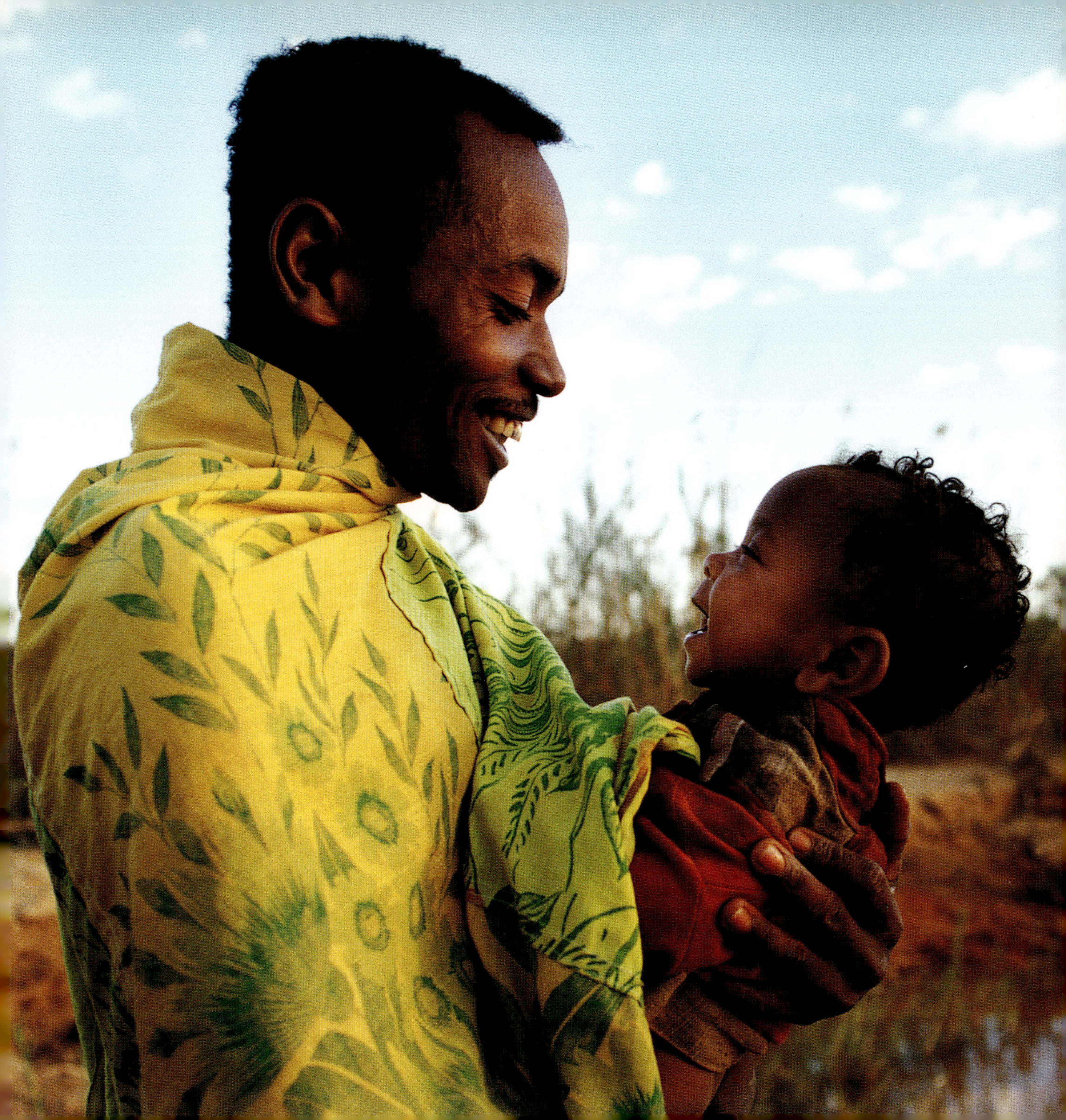

HAPPINESS

MOMENTS INTIMACY LAUGHTER KINSHIP

HODDER

M·I·L·K

MOMENTS INTIMACY LAUGHTER KINSHIP

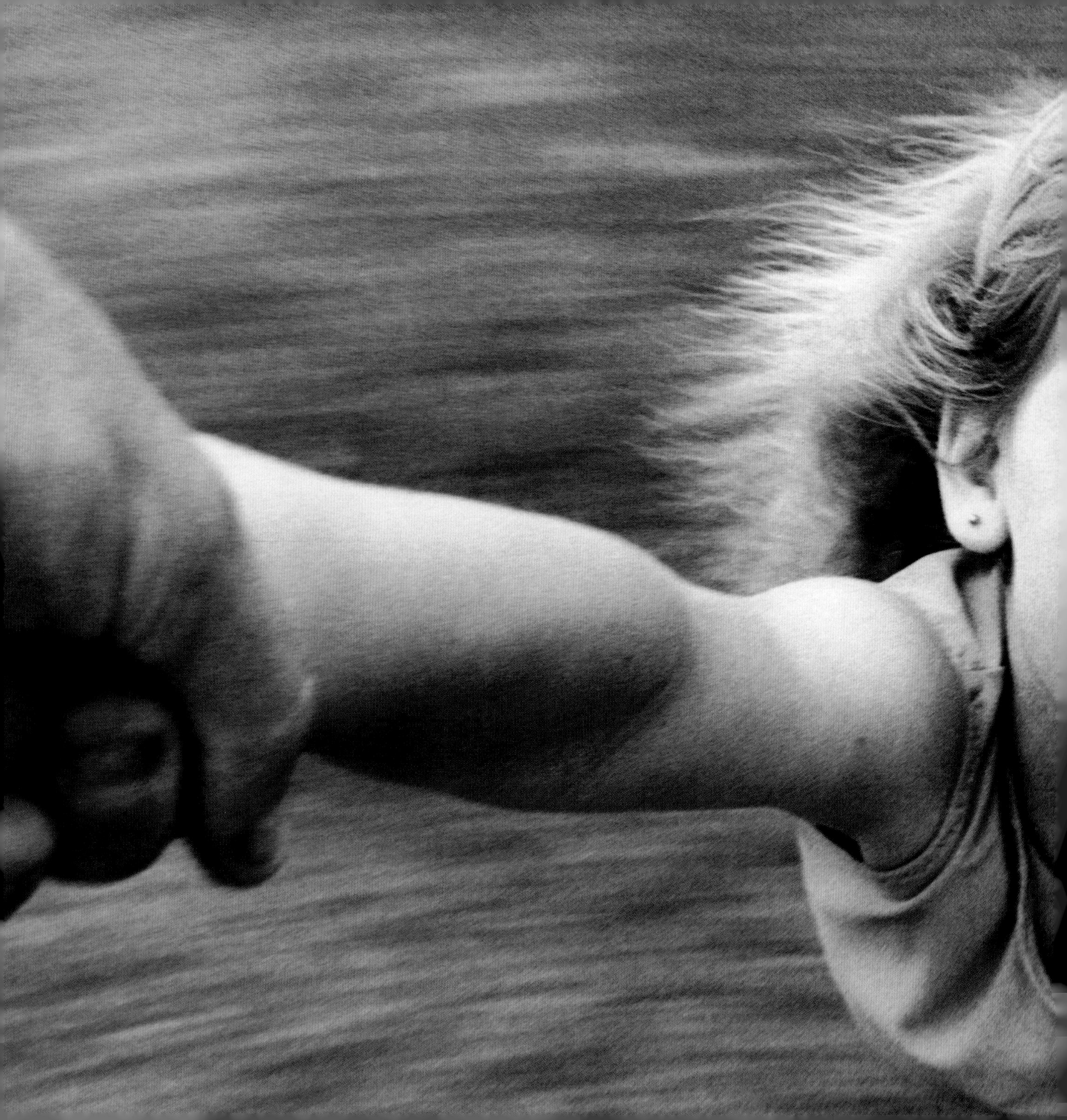

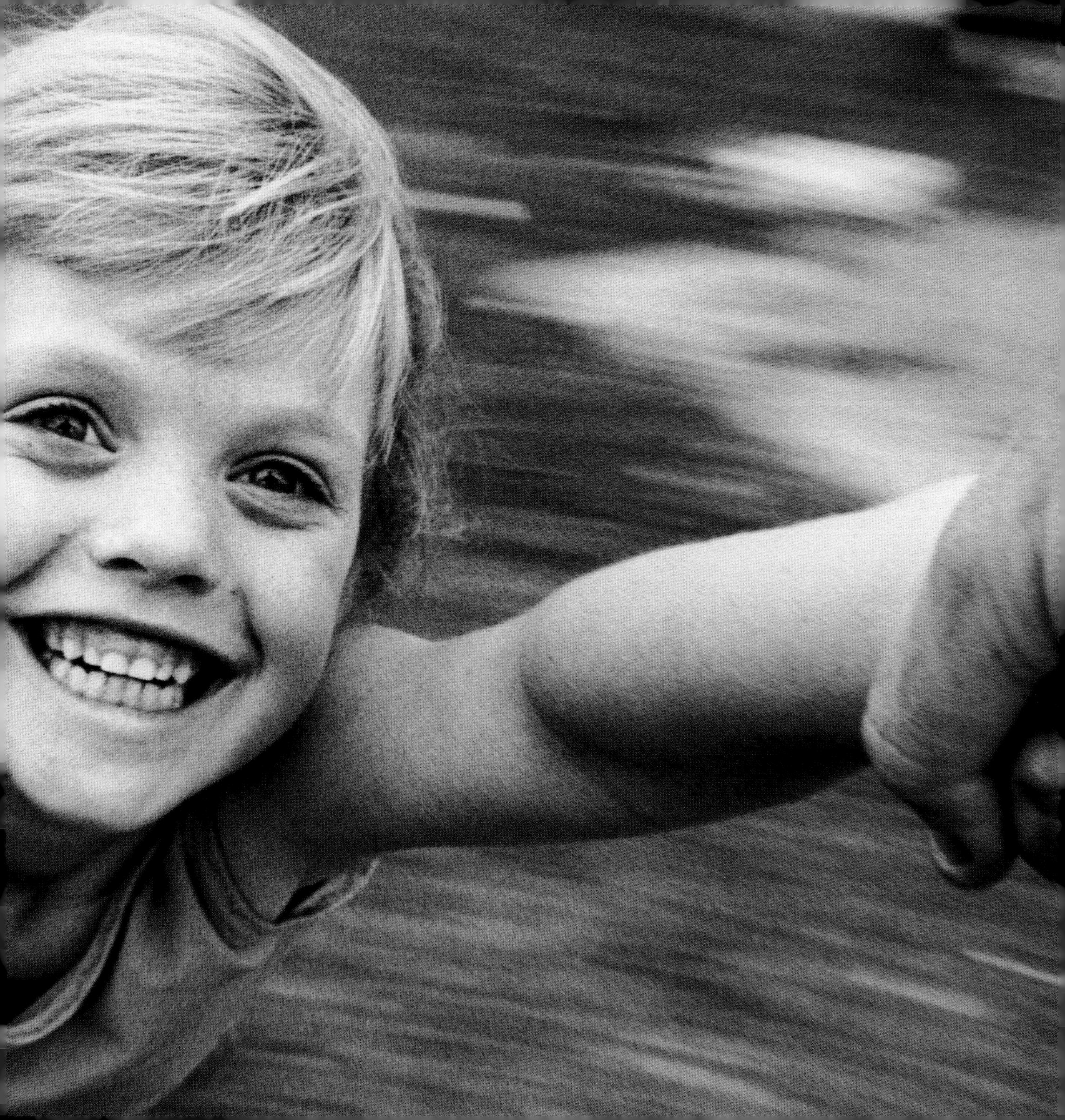

A celebration
of what it is to be part of a family,
to share the gift of friendship
and, more than anything else,
to be loved.

The images in this book were selected from the winners of a competition that involved 17,000 photographers from 164 countries. Over 40,000 photographs were submitted – some in lovingly stitched cloth packages, others alongside warm and heartfelt messages of support and encouragement – unforgettable images of human life, from its first fragile moments to its last.

The competition was called M.I.L.K. – Moments of Intimacy, Laughter and Kinship. It was created to celebrate what it is to be part of a family, to share the gift of friendship and, more than anything else, to be loved.

And so the images are here for you to enjoy. My hope is that you will look through this book and recognise the people in it. Their moments are our moments. The instants of their lives, captured here, are universal. These images speak to all of us with clarity, universality and – to use that elusive and neglected word – joy.

I hope you enjoy your journey through these pages. All these moments of intimacy, laughter and kinship belong to you.

Geoff Blackwell M.I.L.K.

Innocence is the child, and forgetfulness, **a new beginning**,
a game, a self-rolling wheel, a first movement,
a Holy Yea.

[FRIEDRICH NIETZCHE]

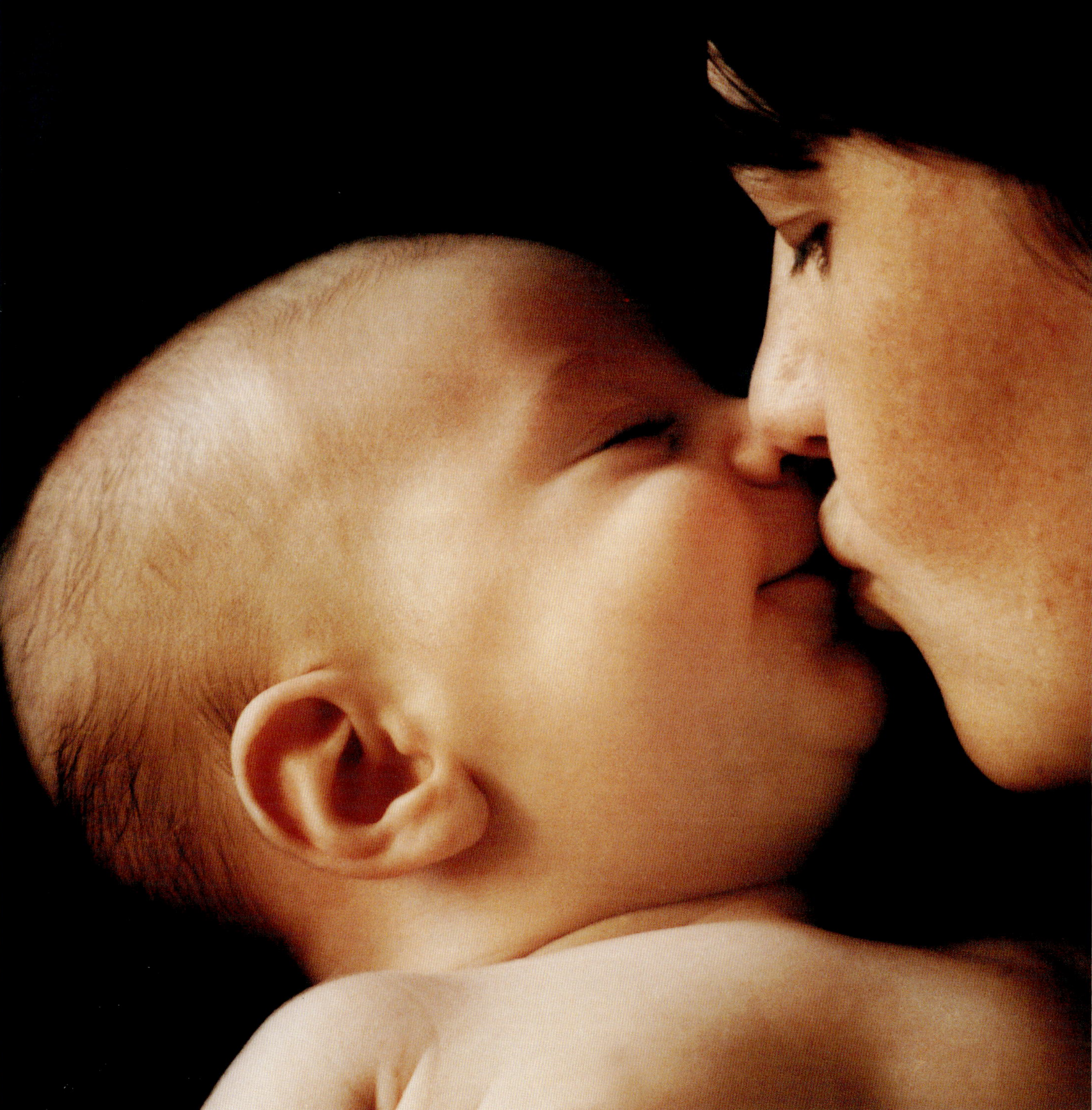

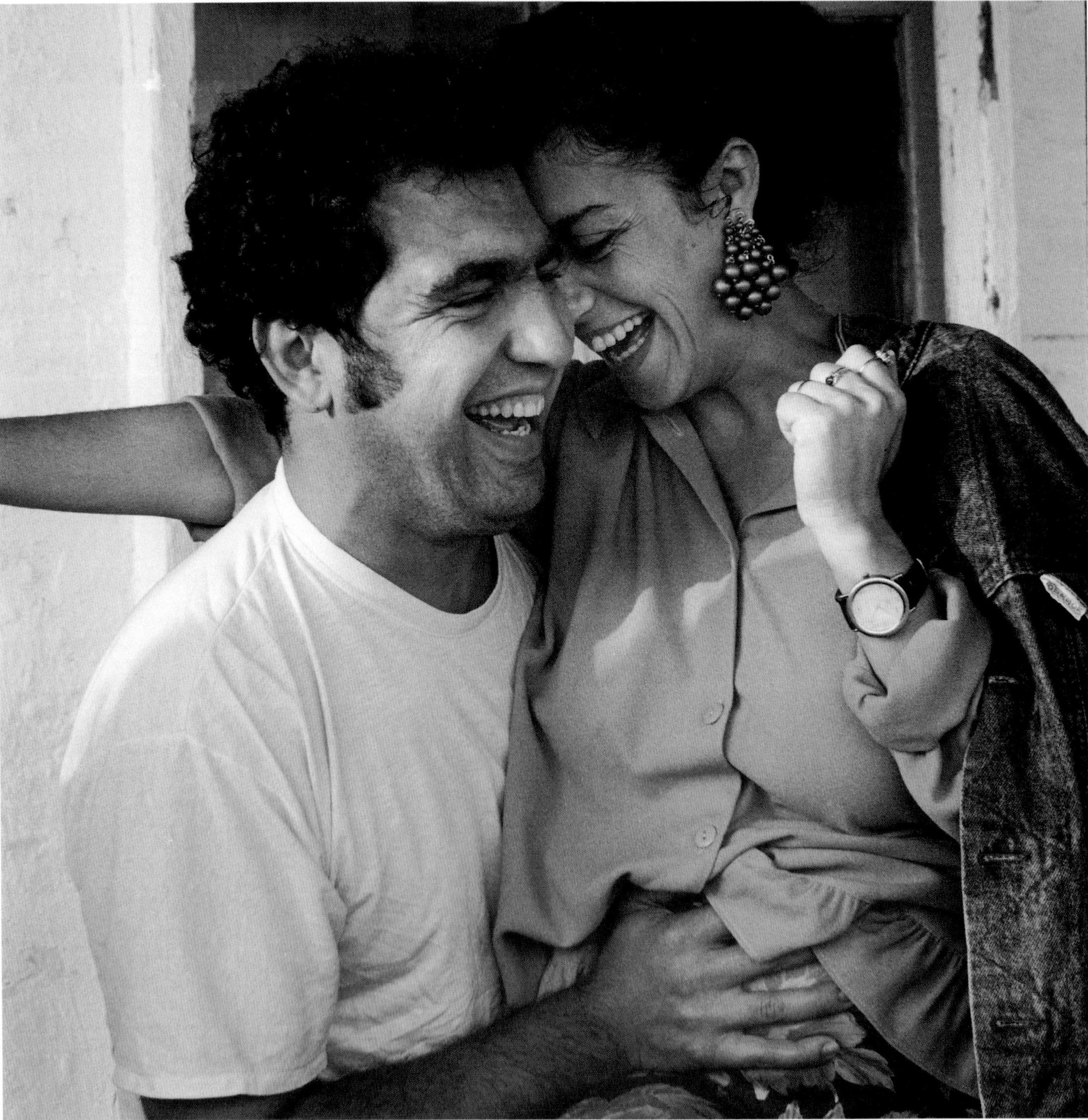

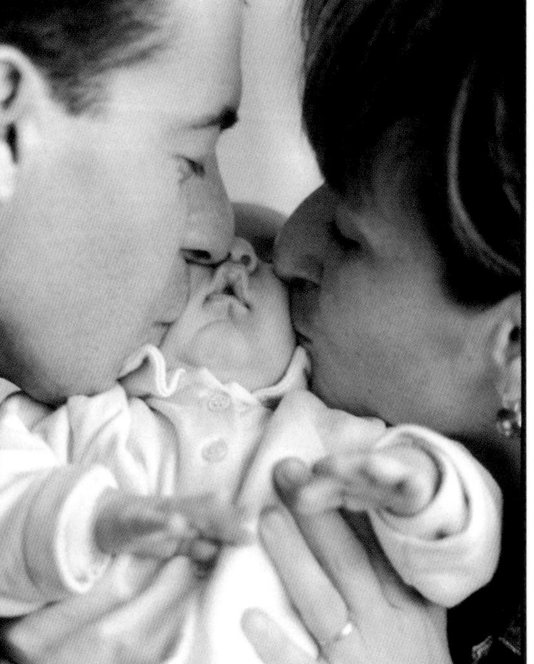

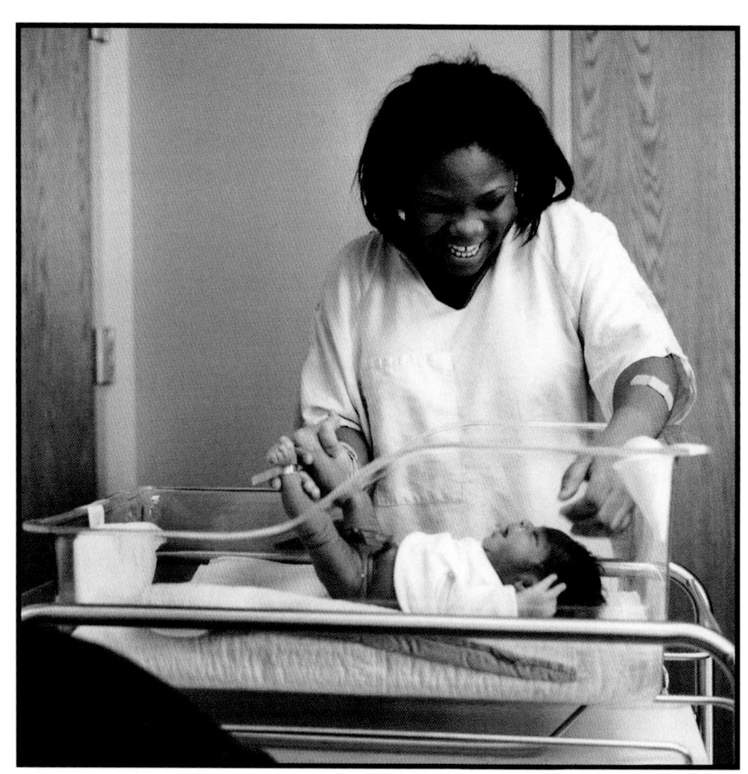

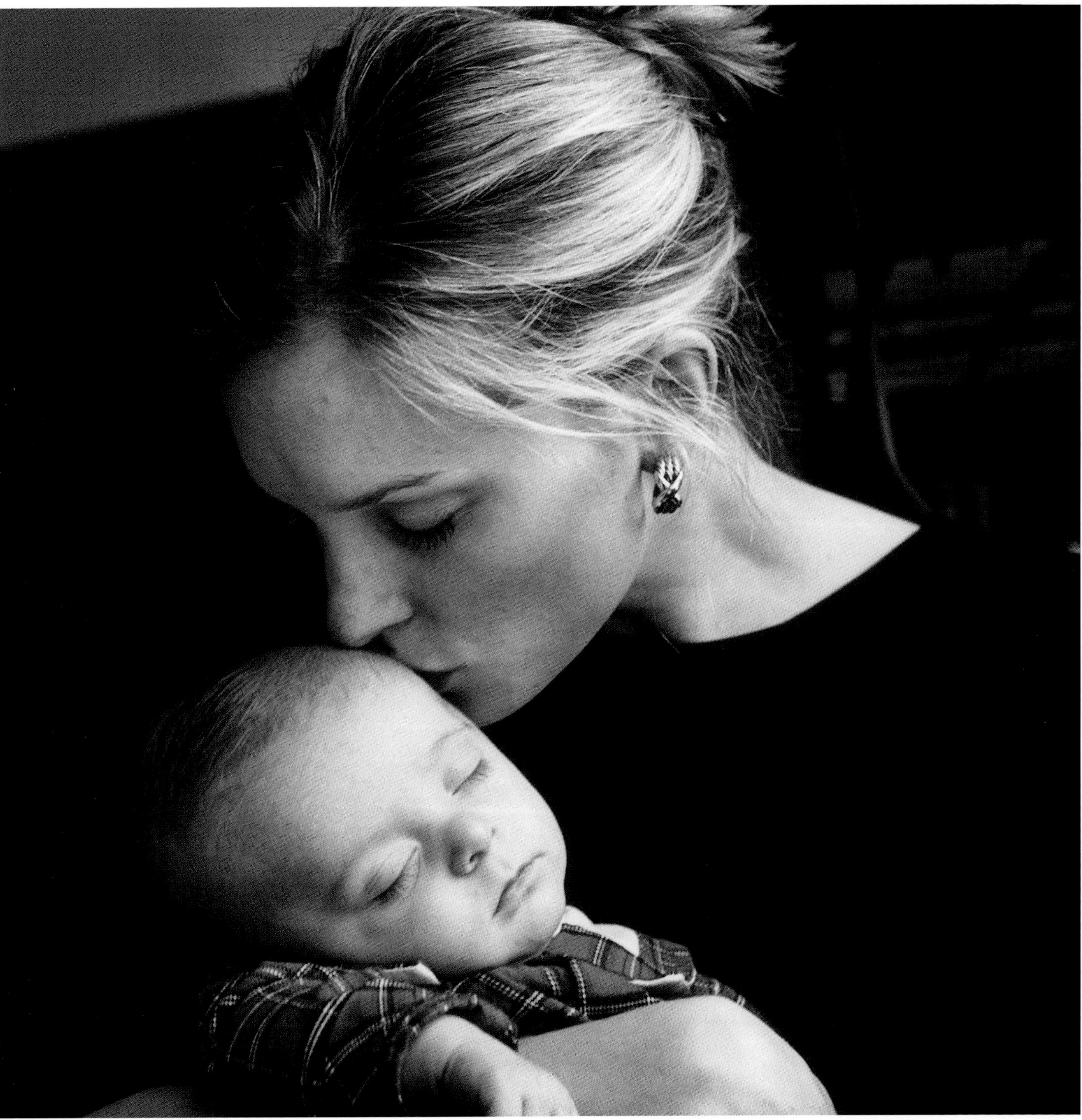

Hold tenderly that which you cherish.

[BOB ALBERTI]

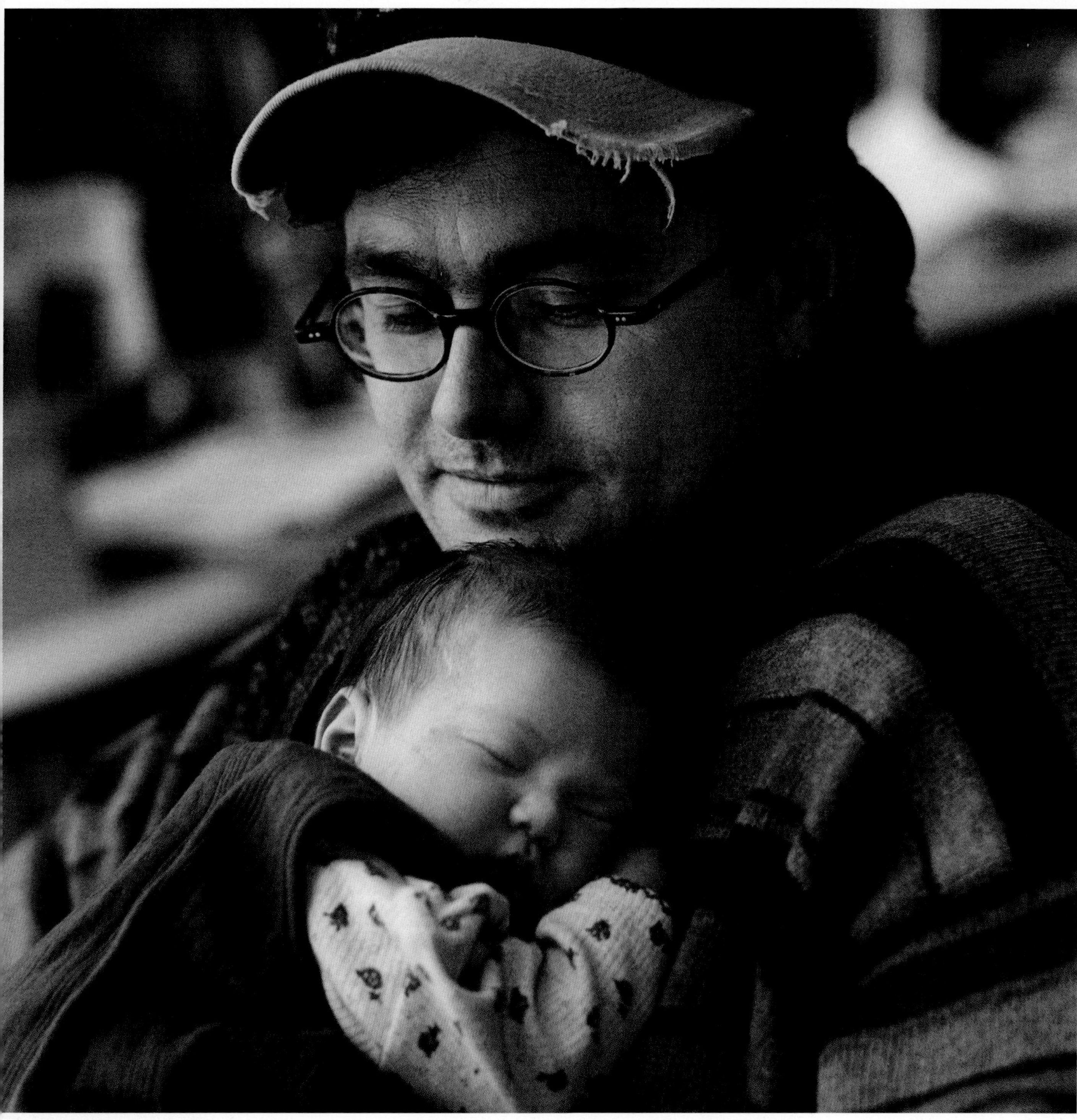

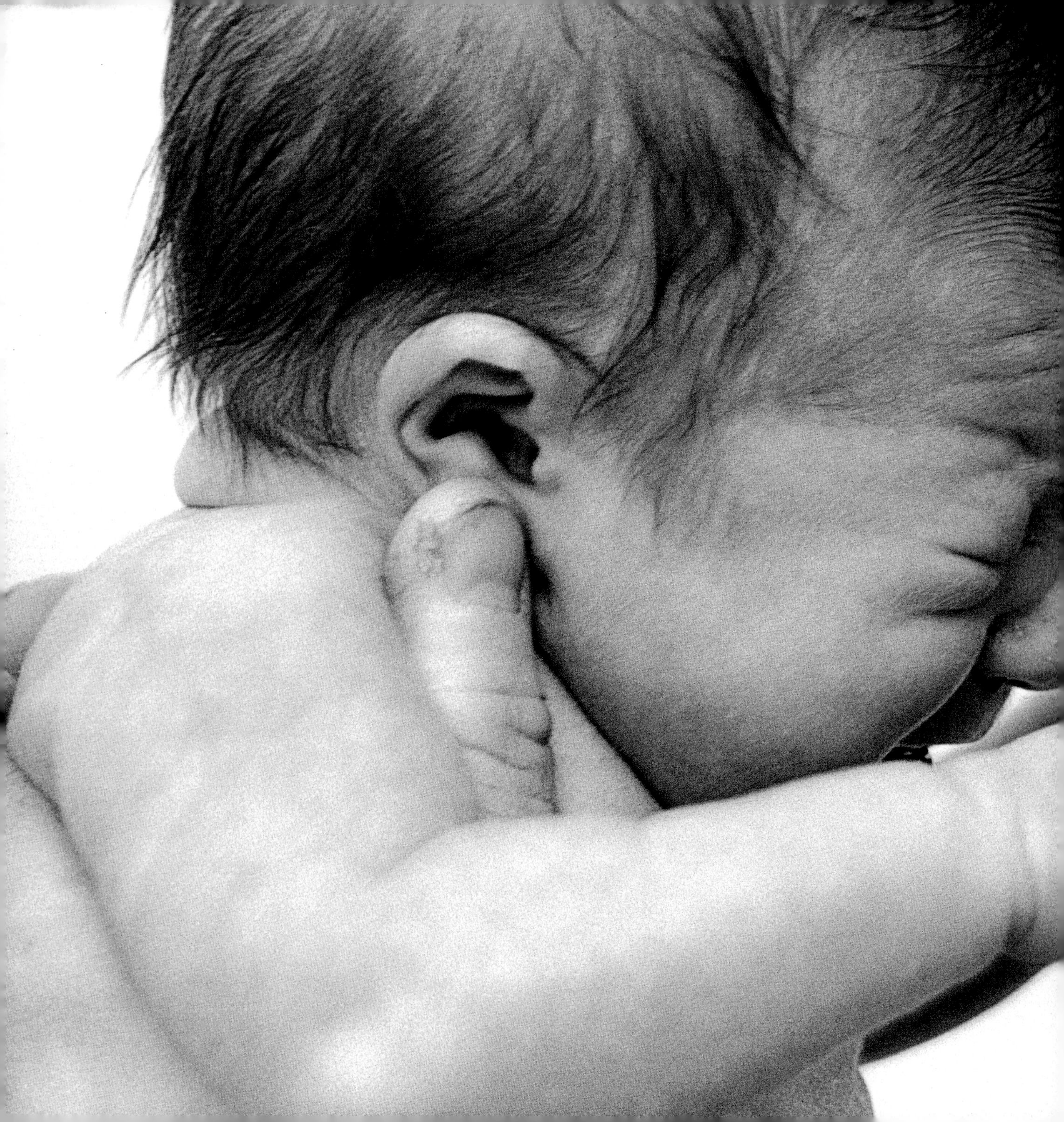

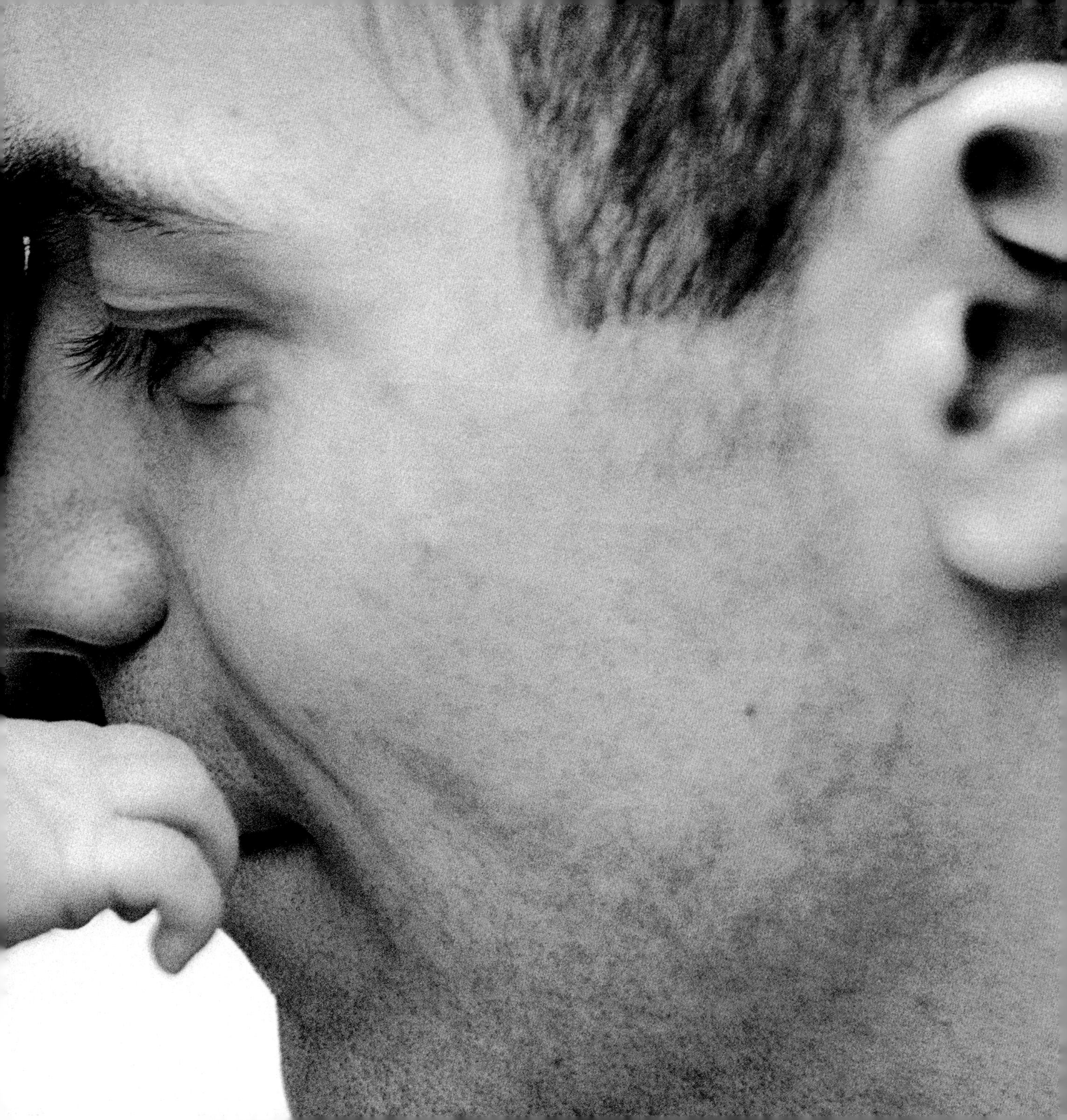

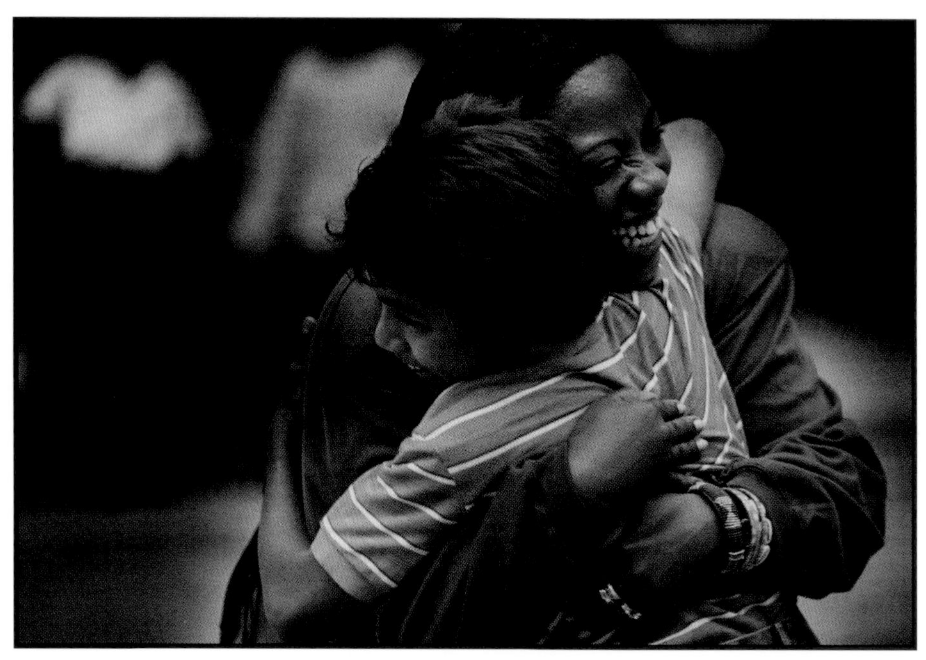

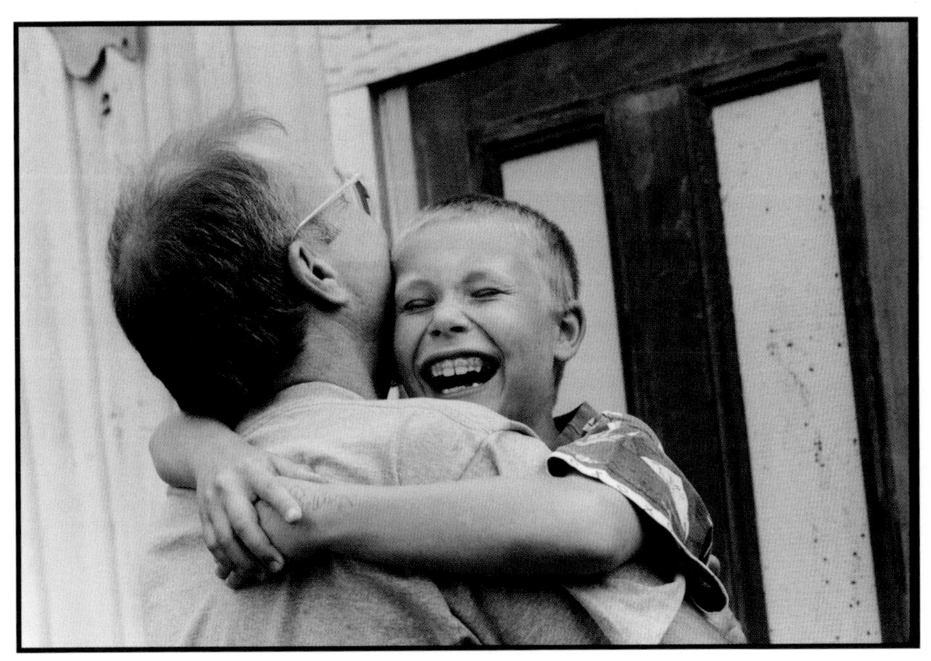

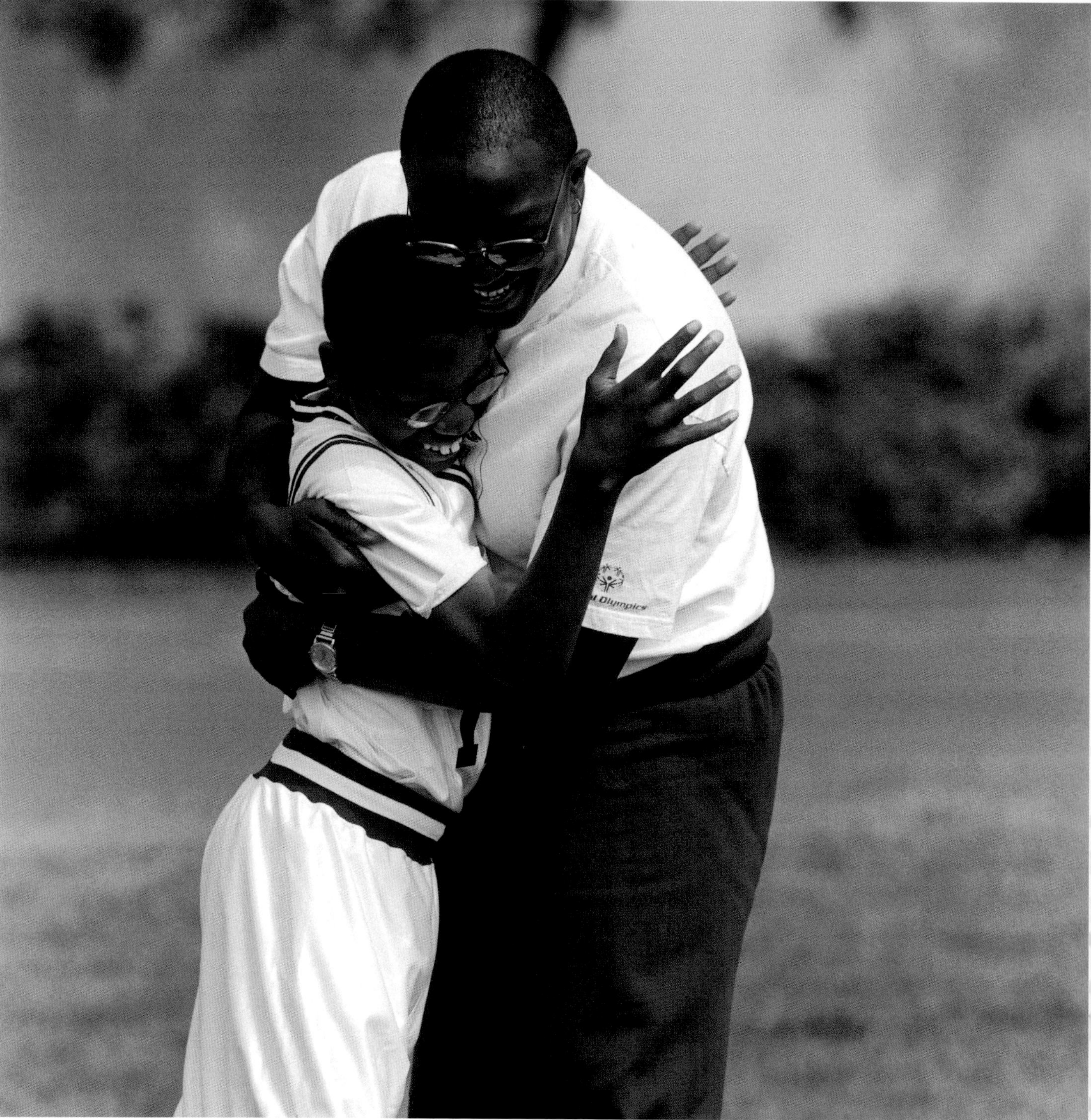
Olympics

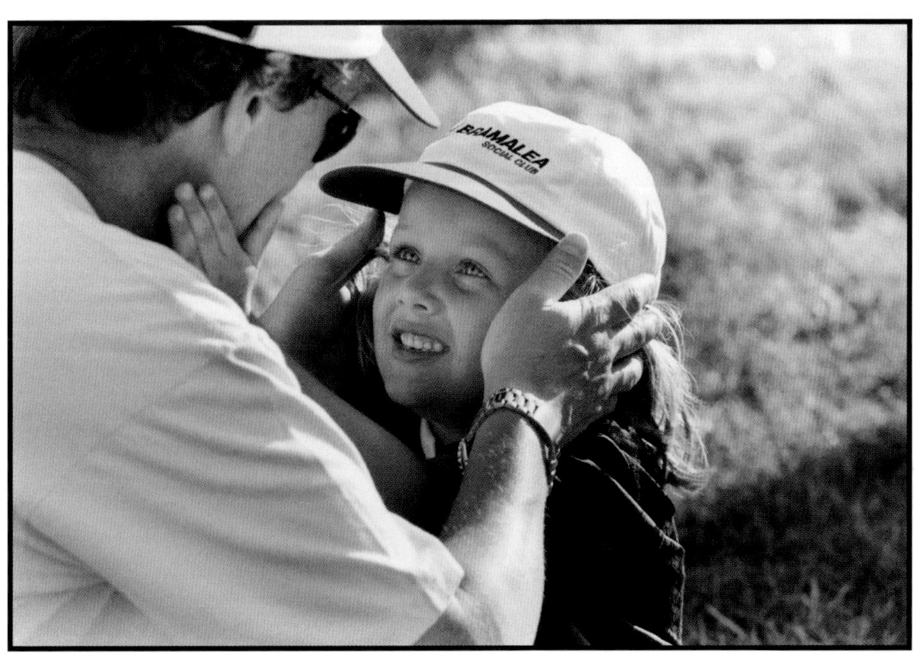
SOCIAL CLUB

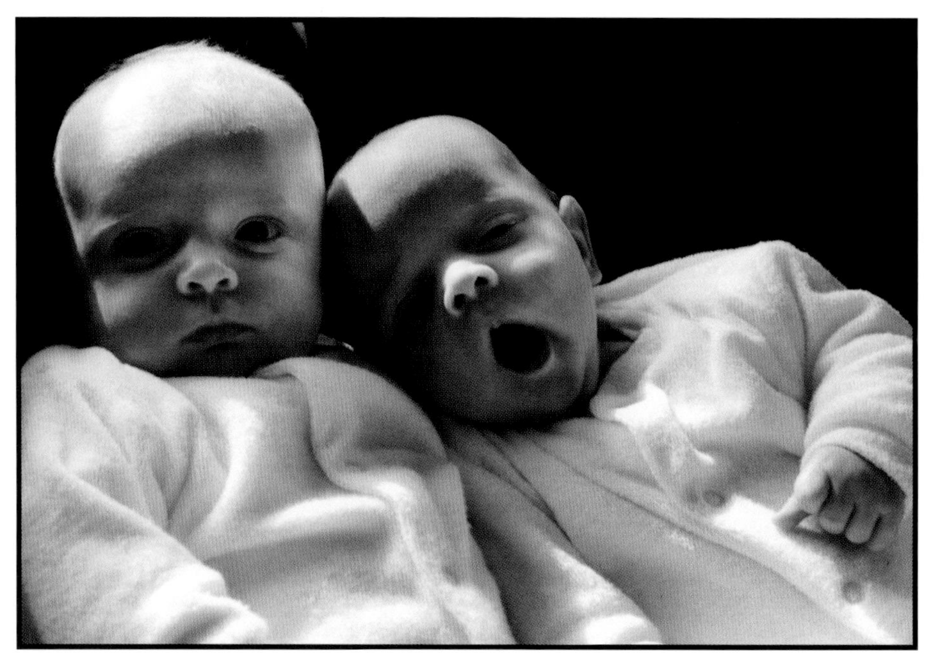

We find delight in the beauty and happiness...

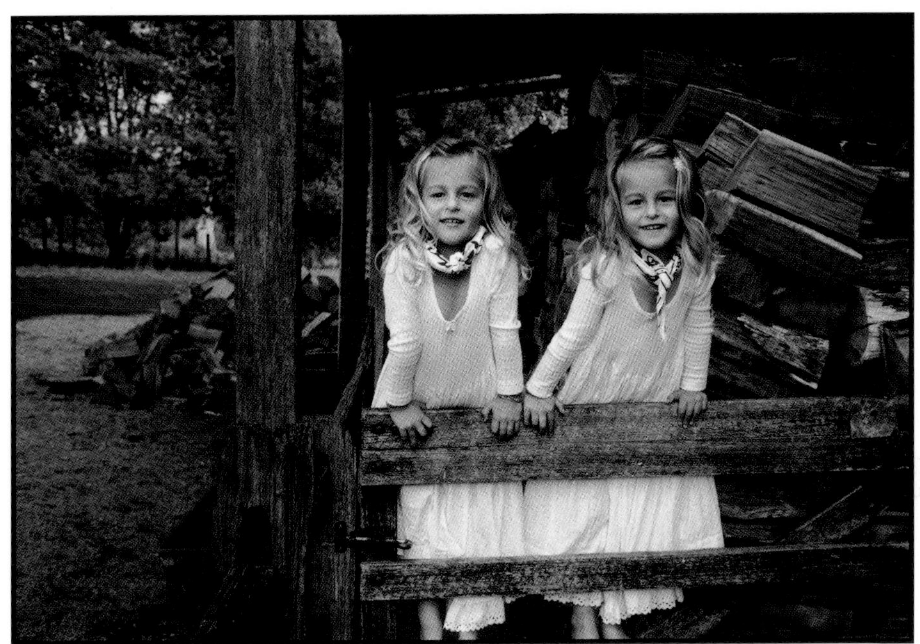

of children that makes the heart too big for the body.

[RALPH WALDO EMERSON]

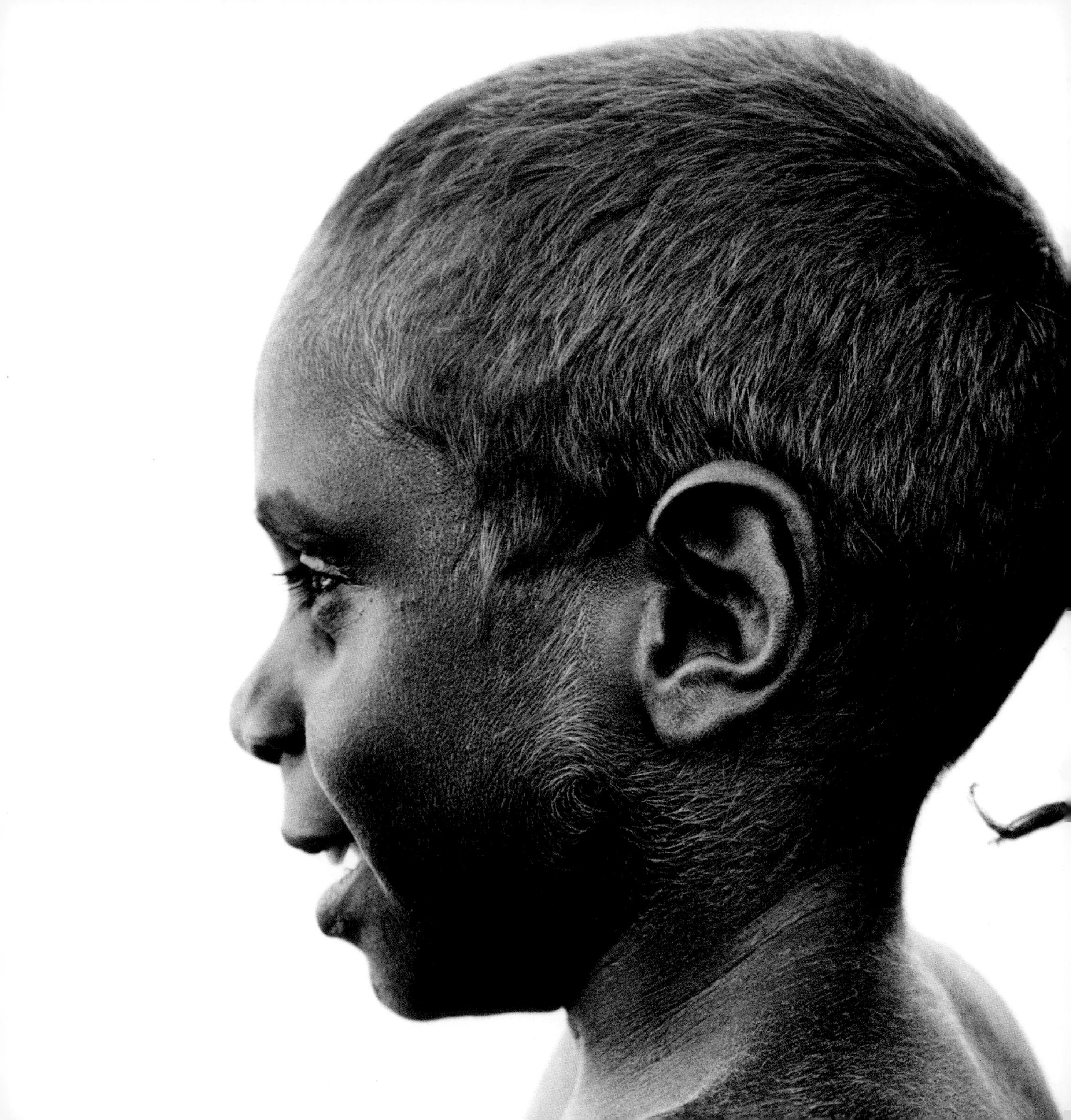

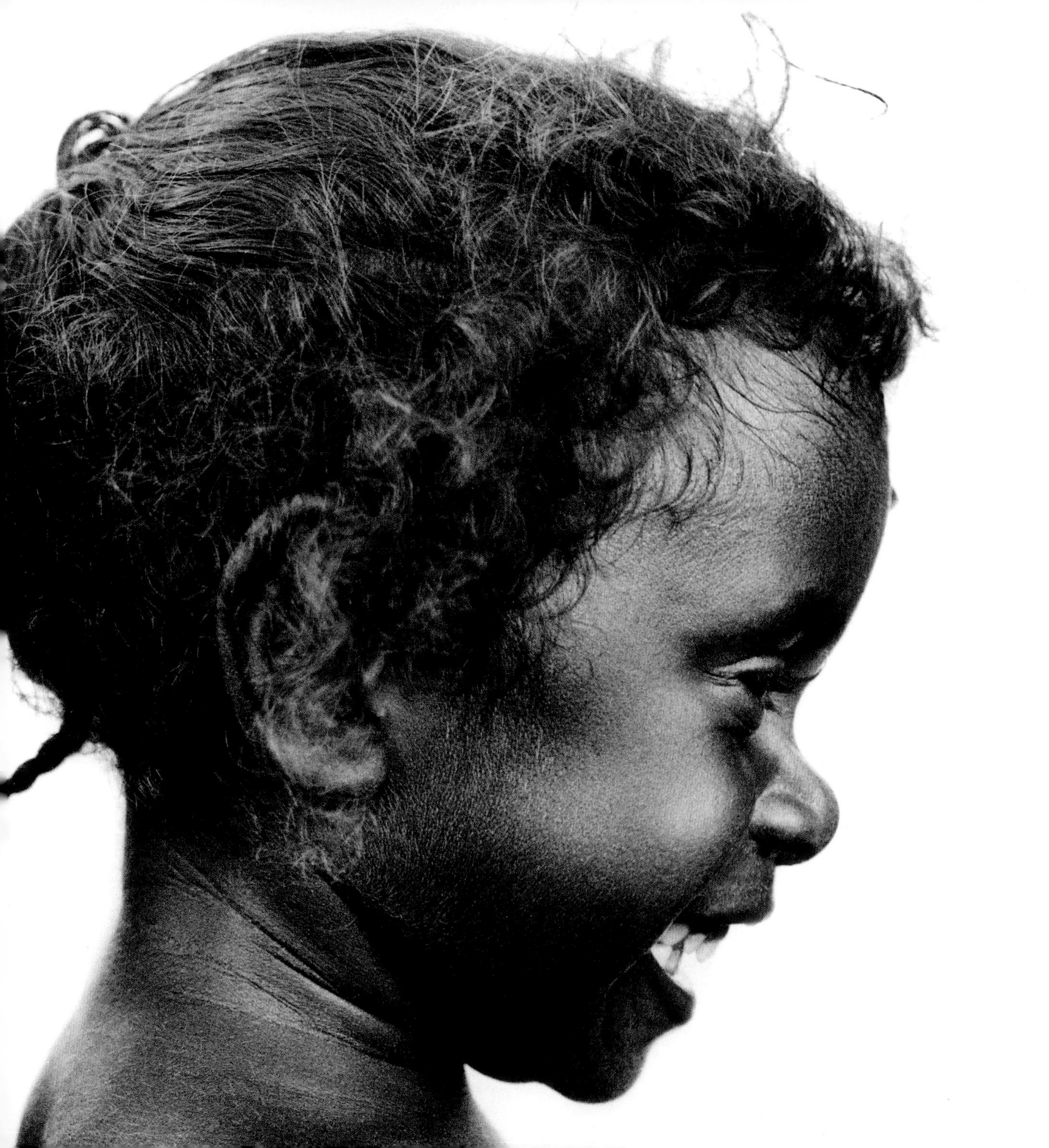

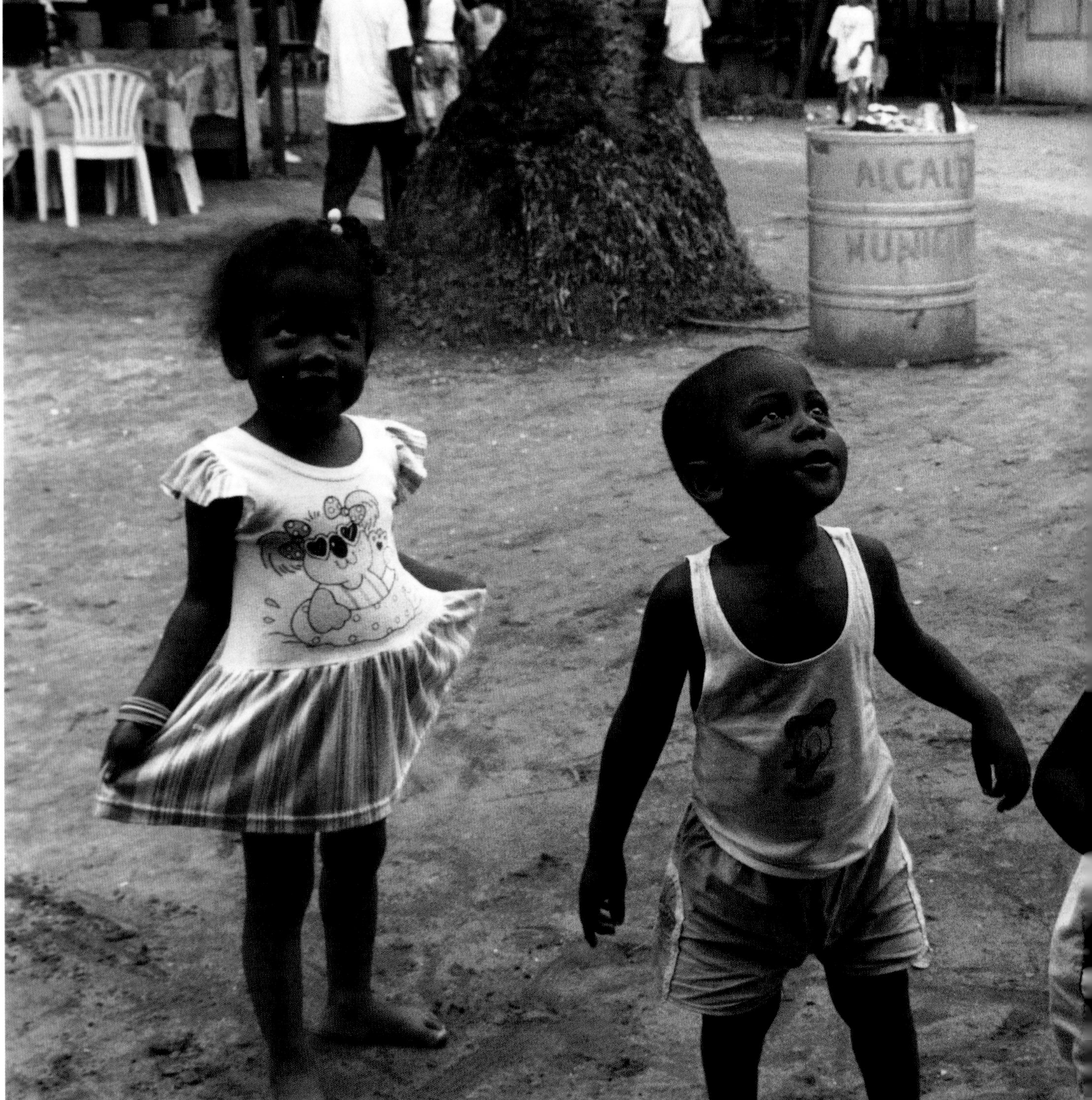

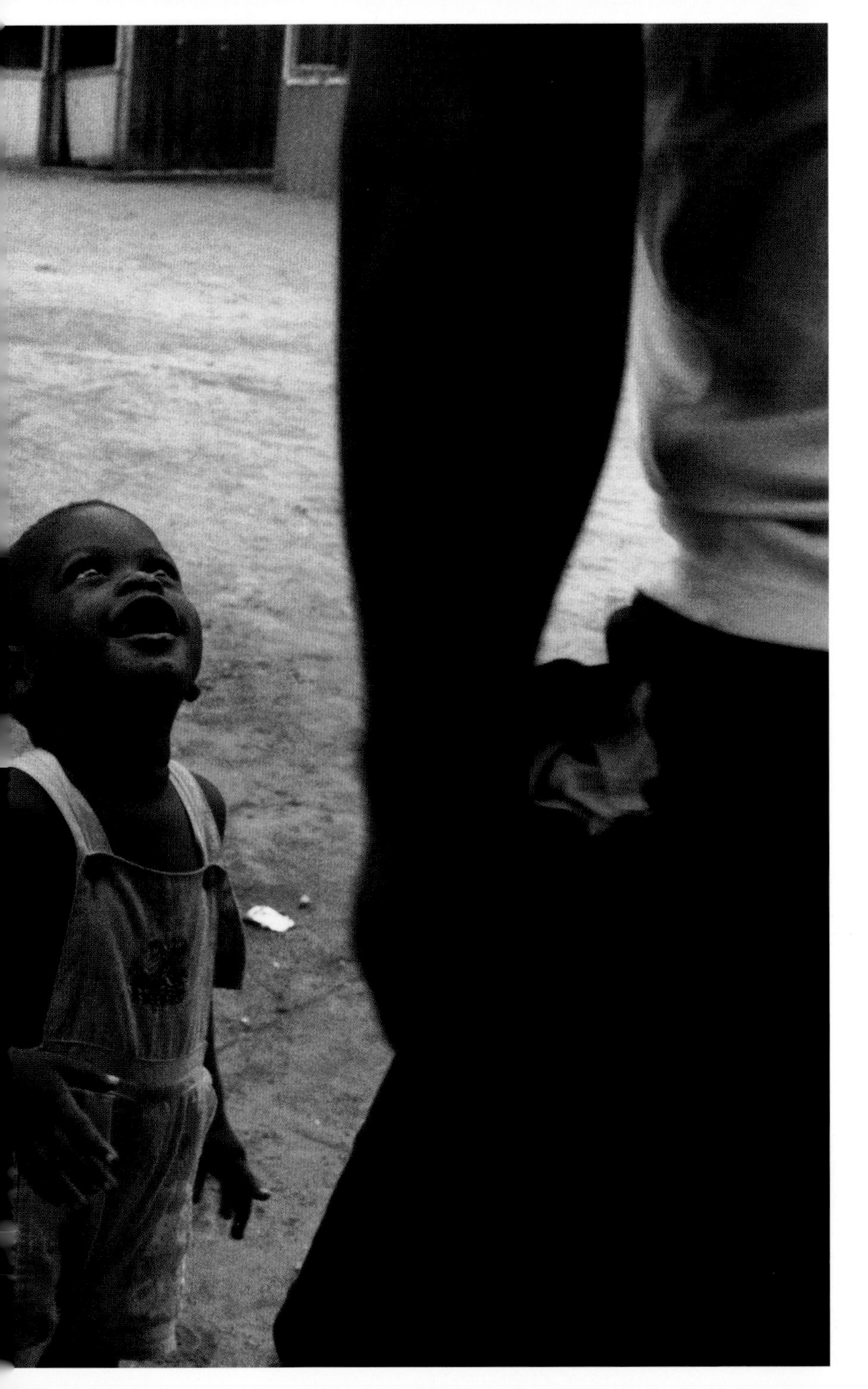

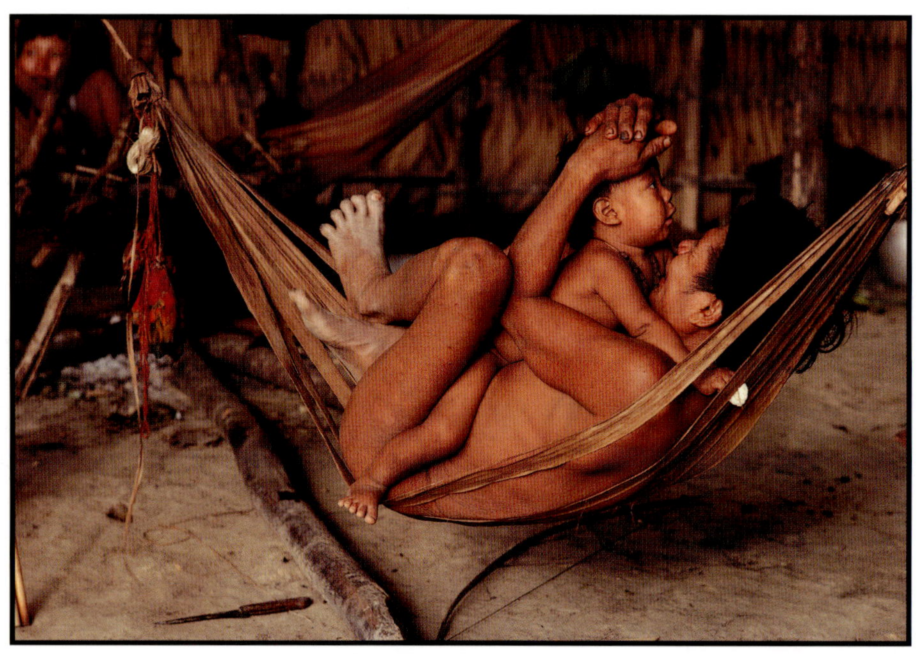

Family faces are magic mirrors.

[GAIL LUMET BUCKLEY]

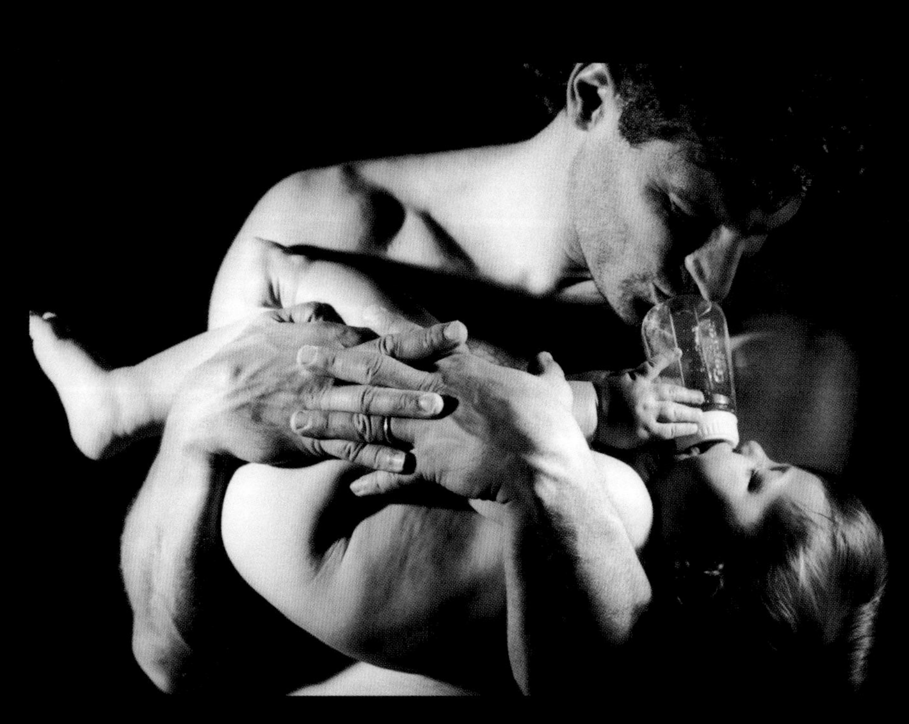

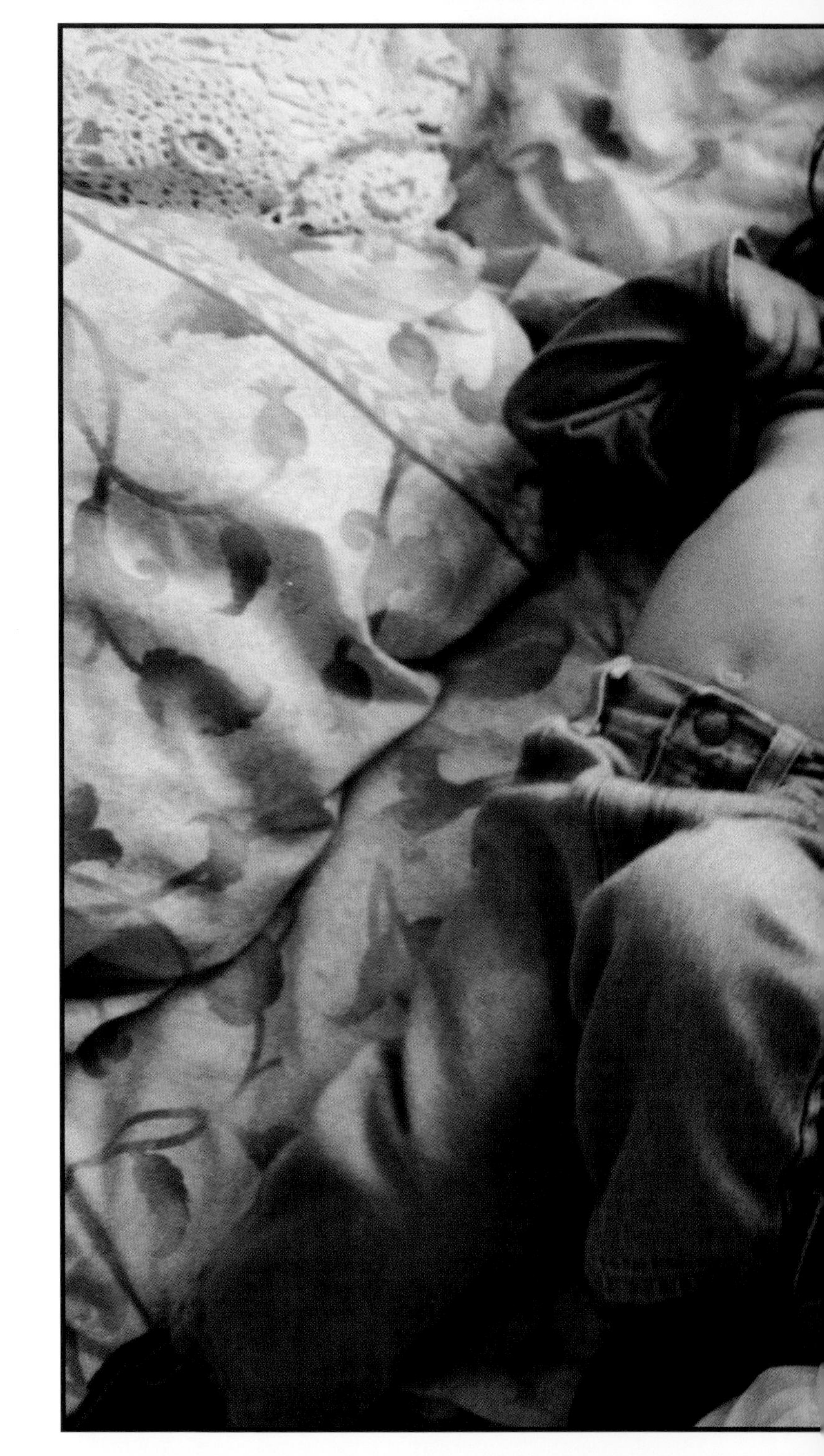

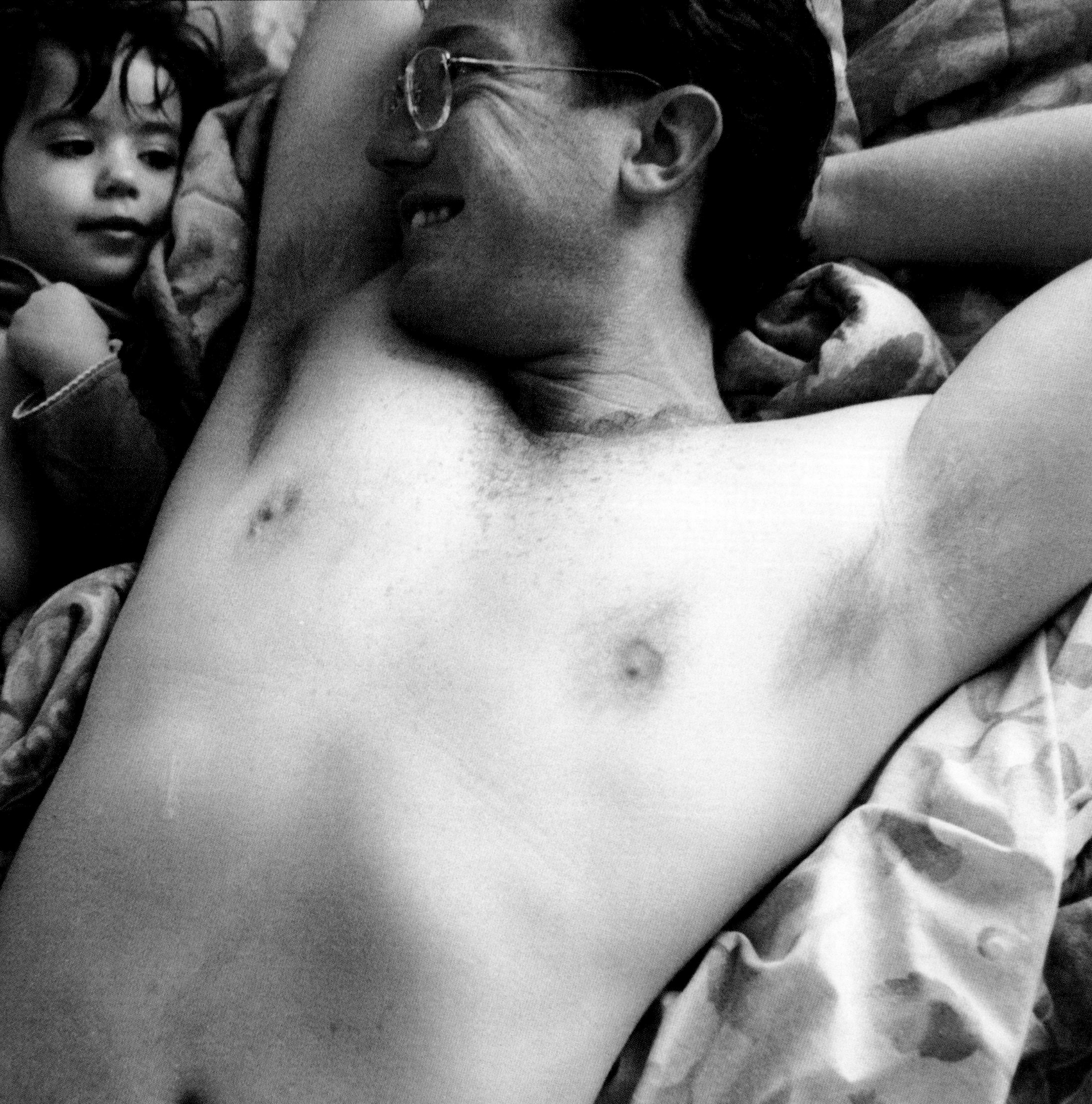

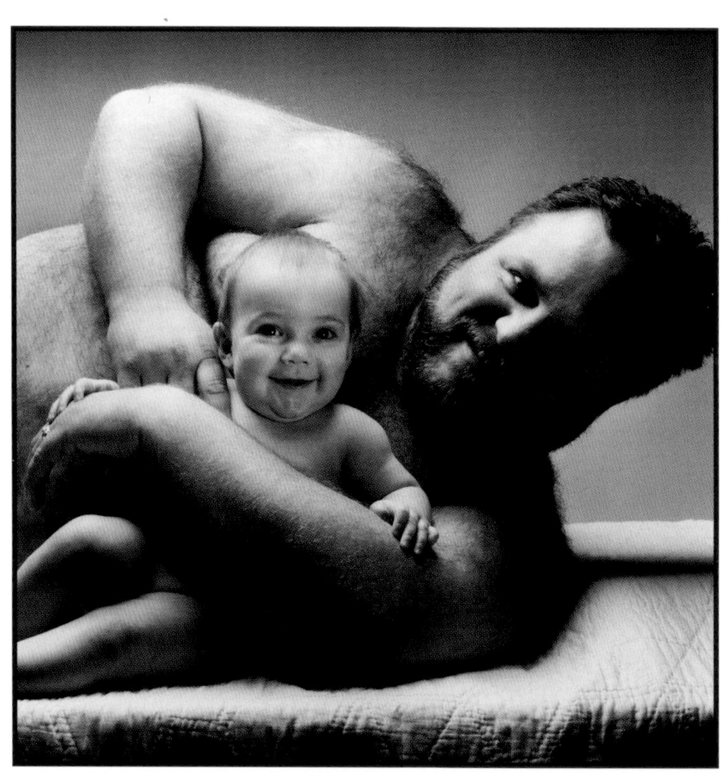

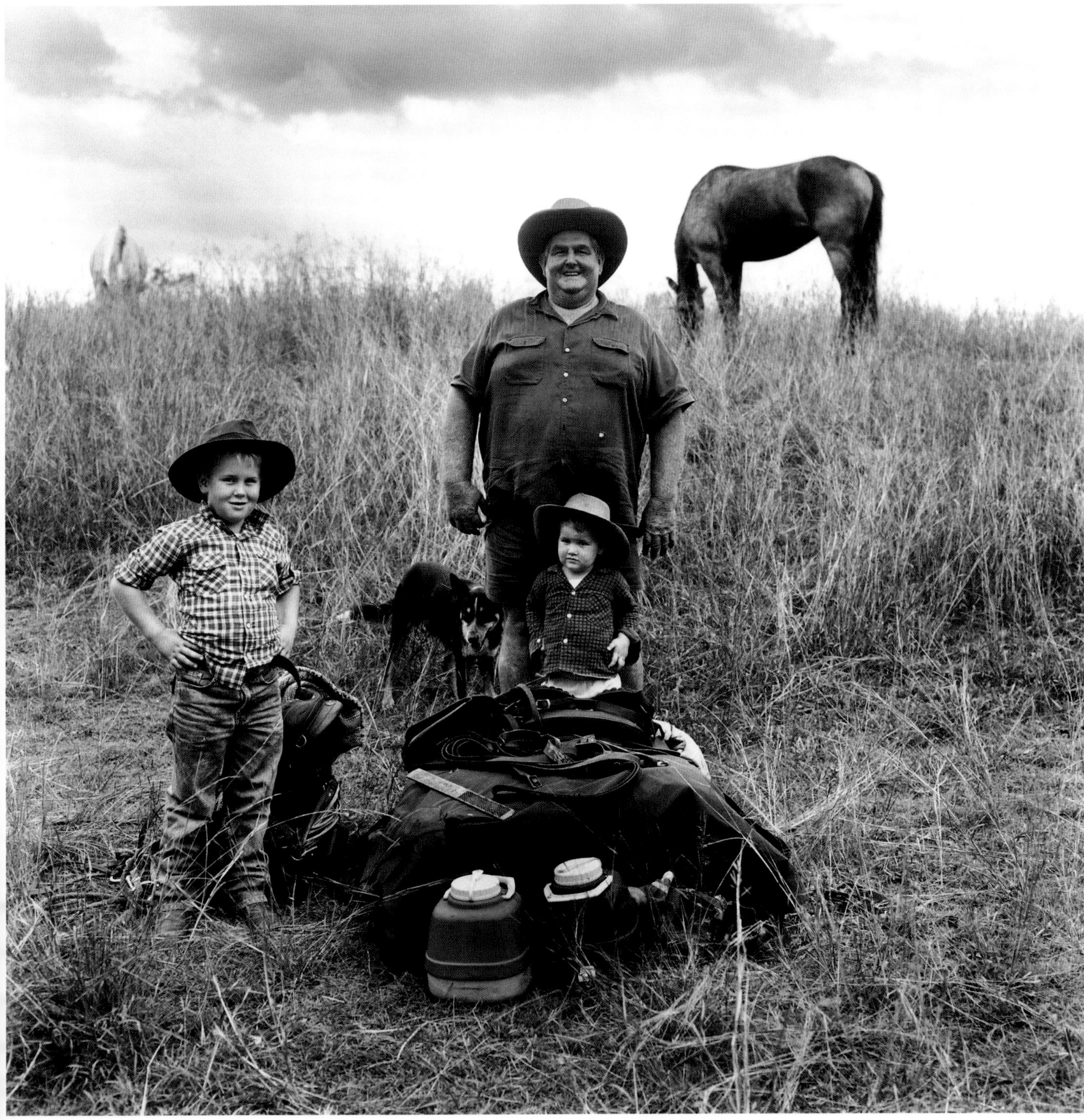

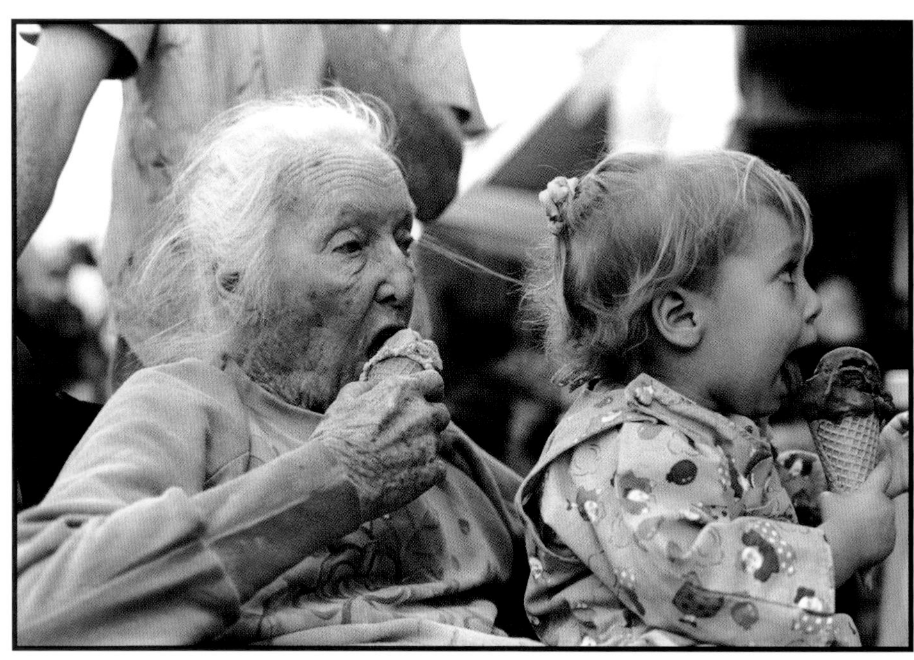

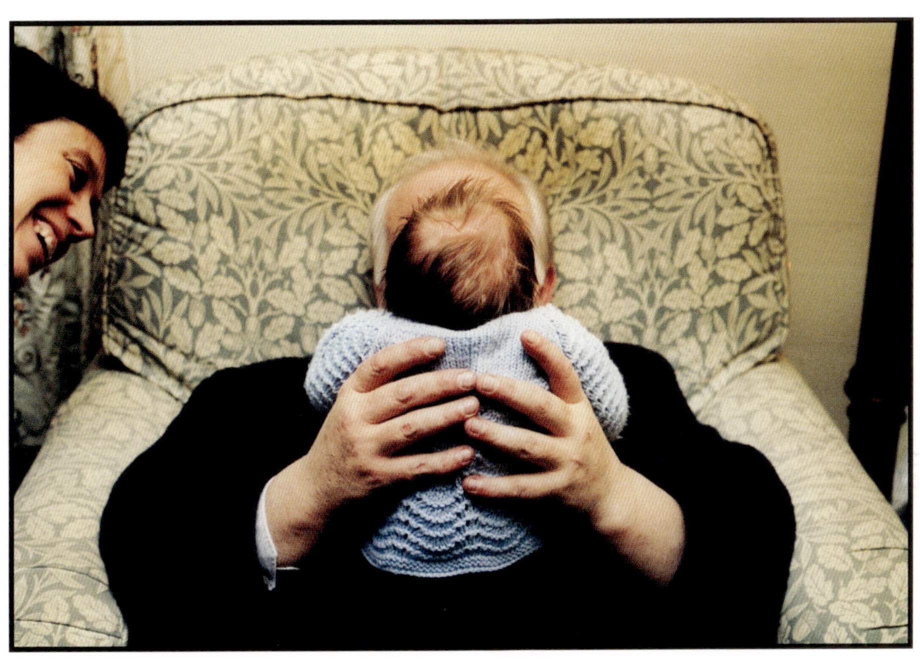

Other things may change us, but we start and end with family.

[ANTHONY BRANDT]

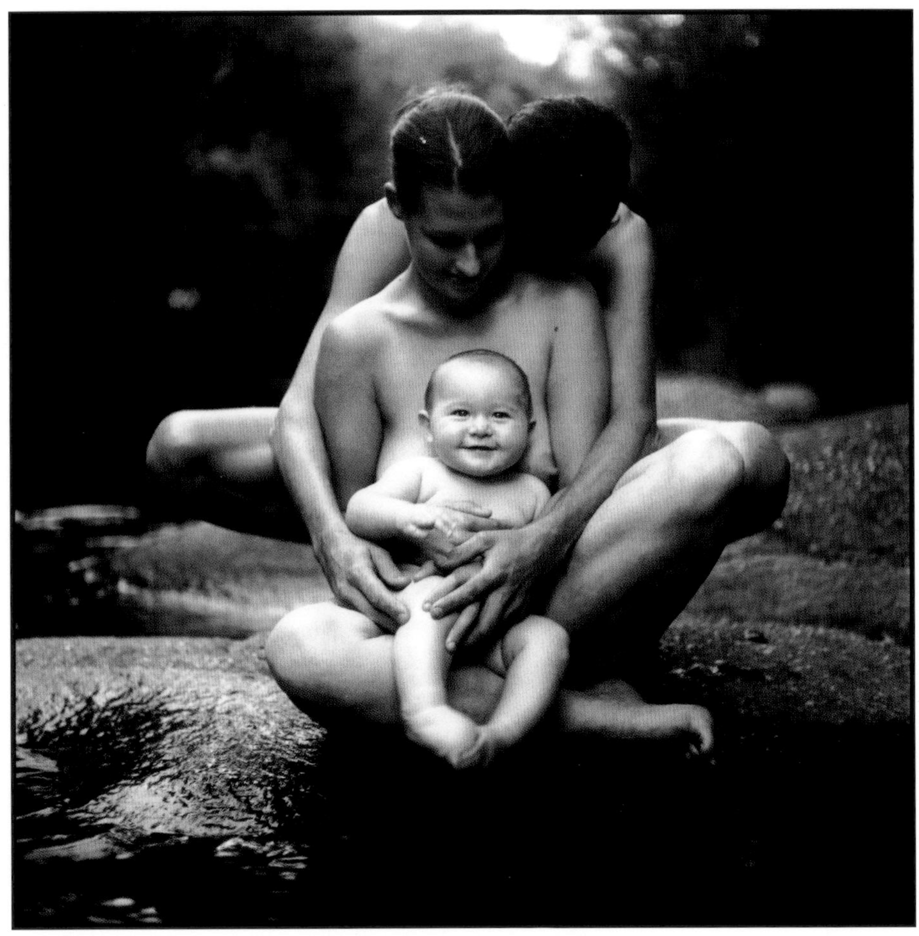

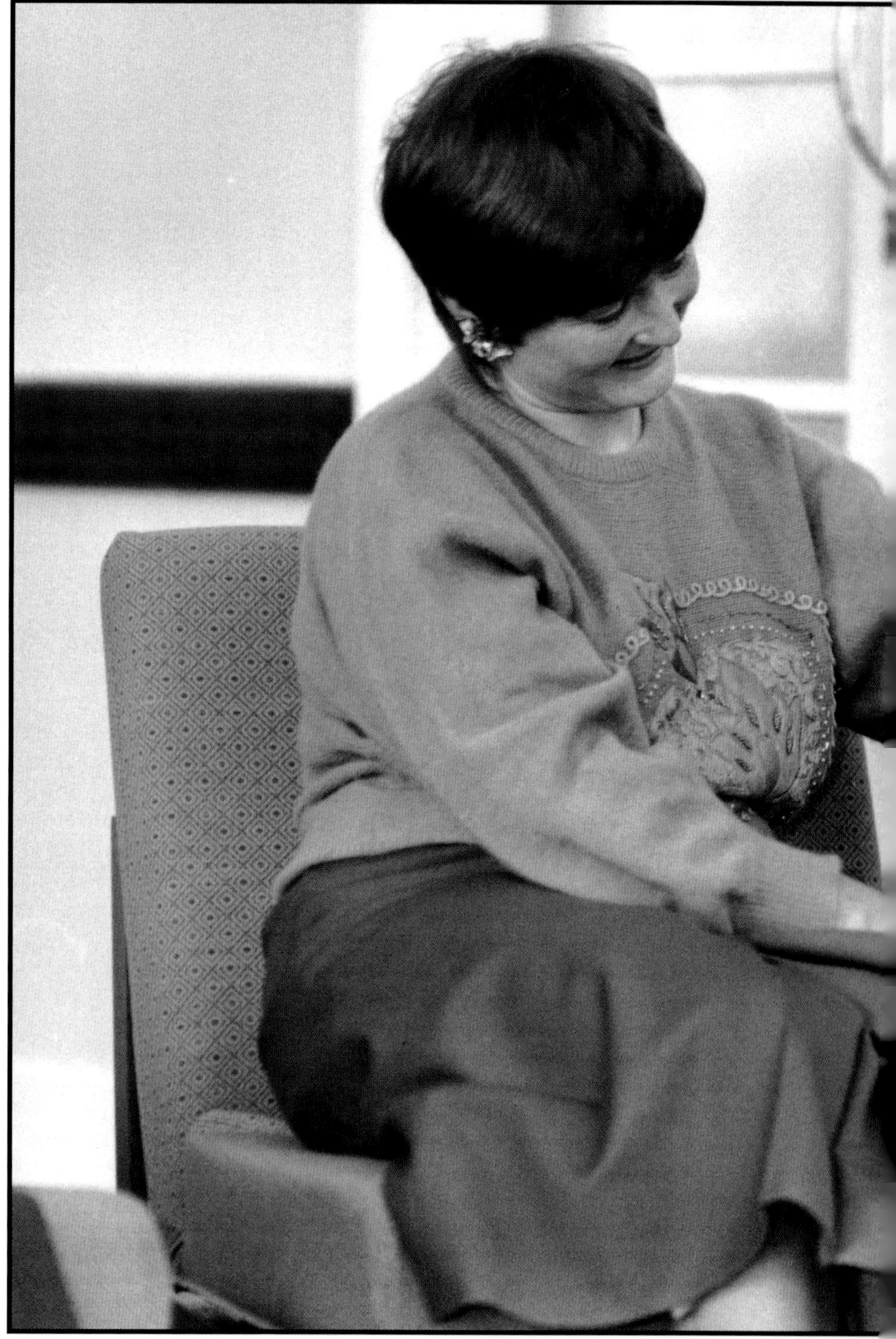

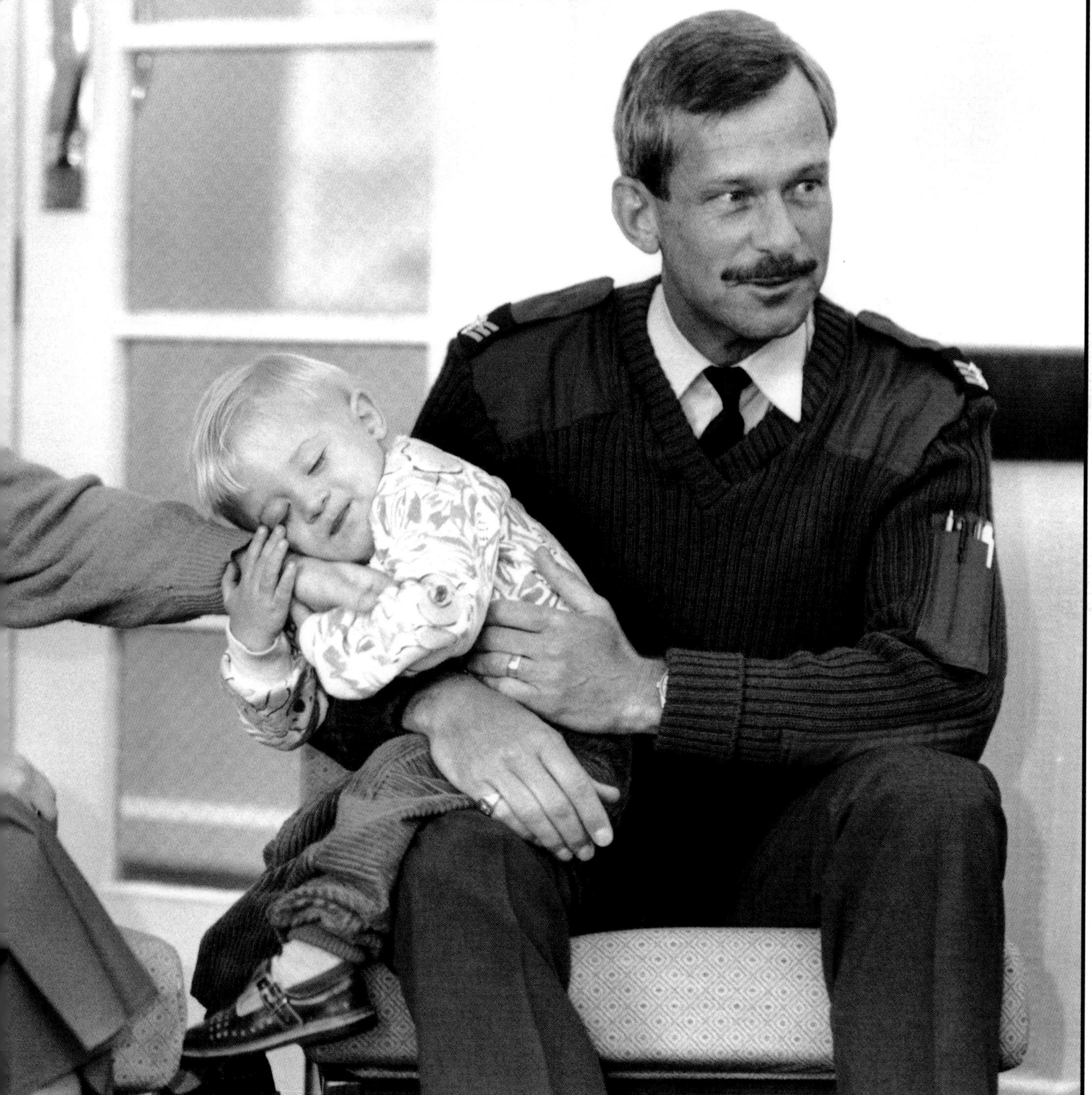

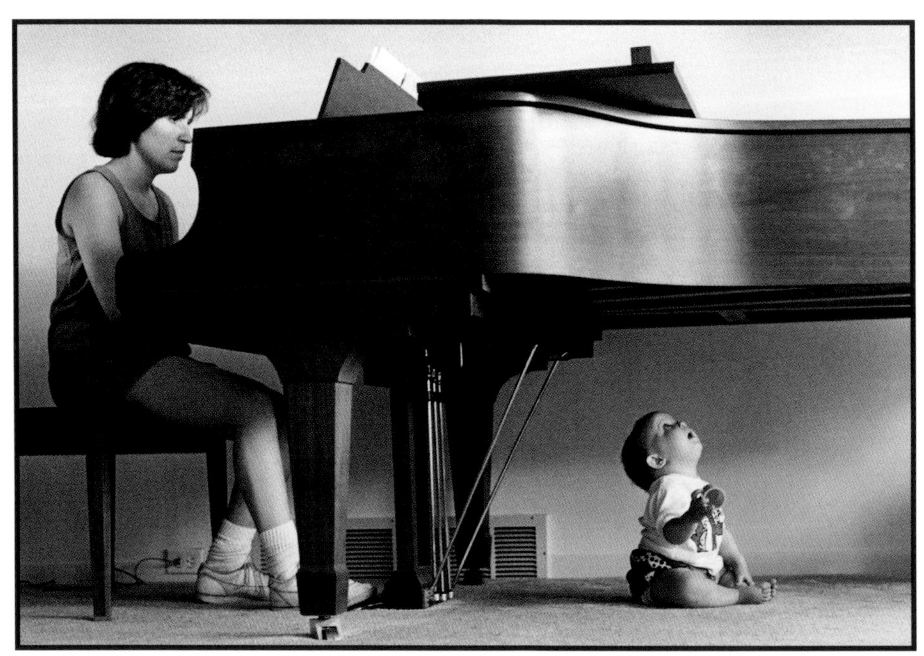

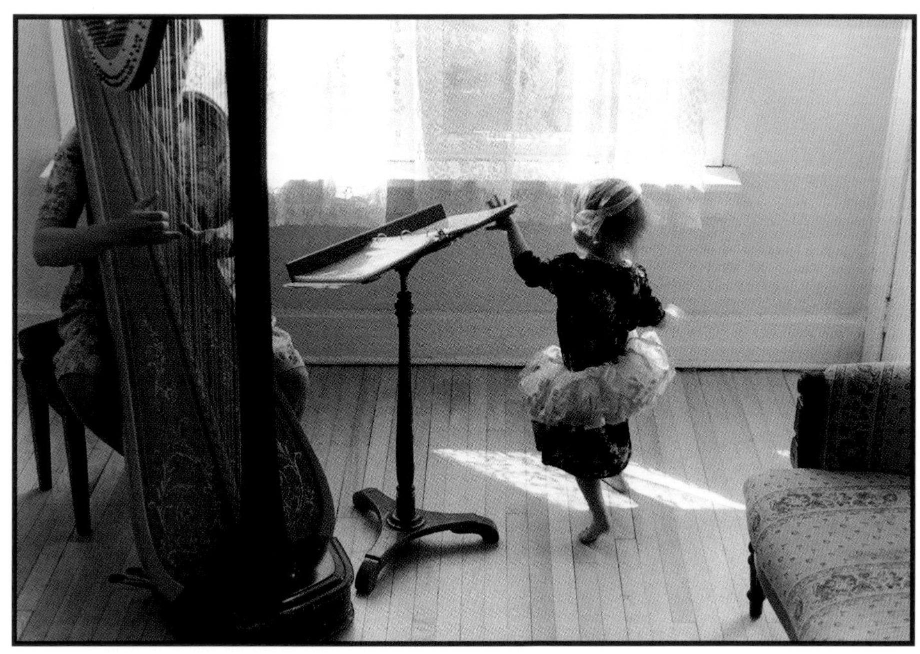

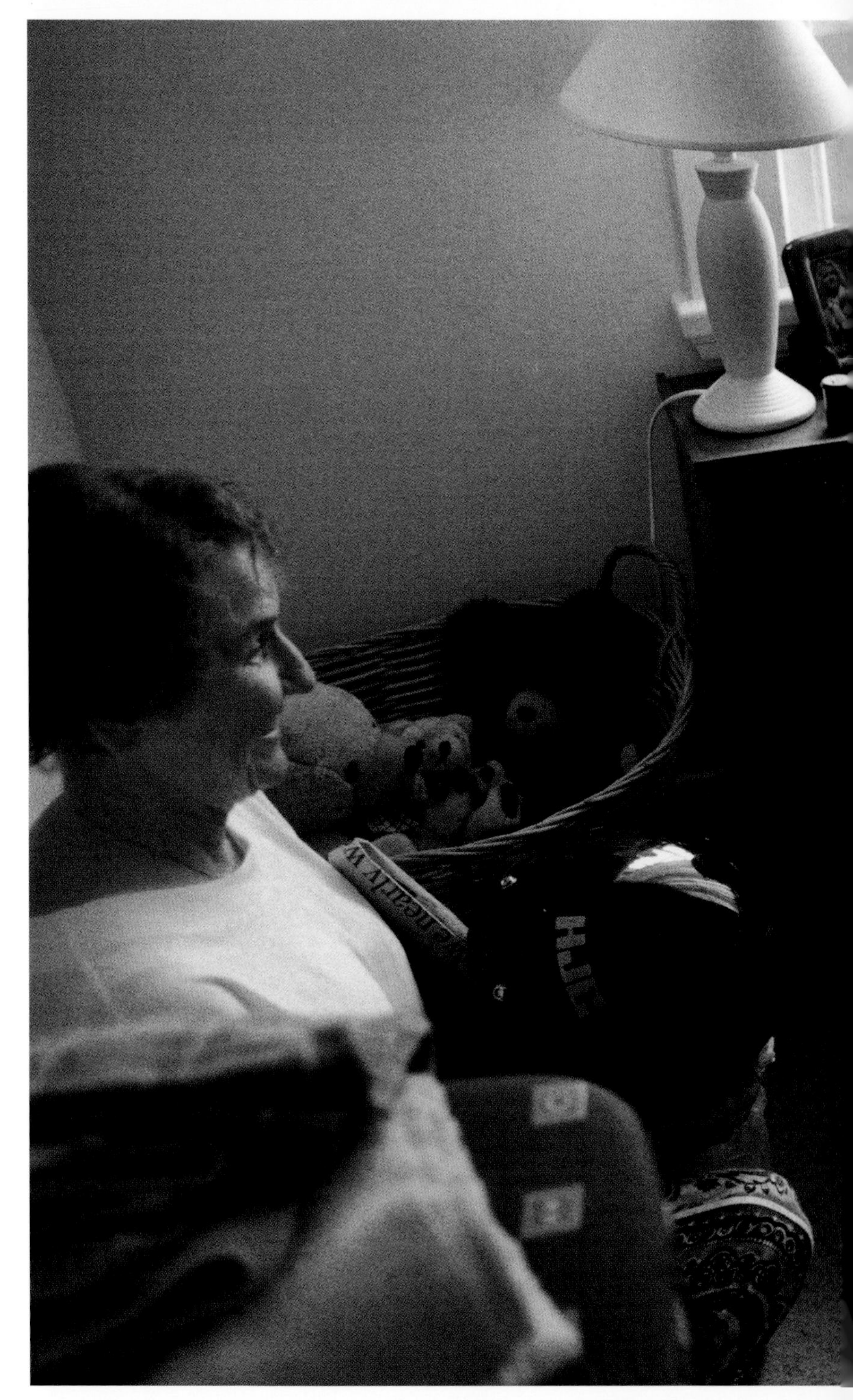

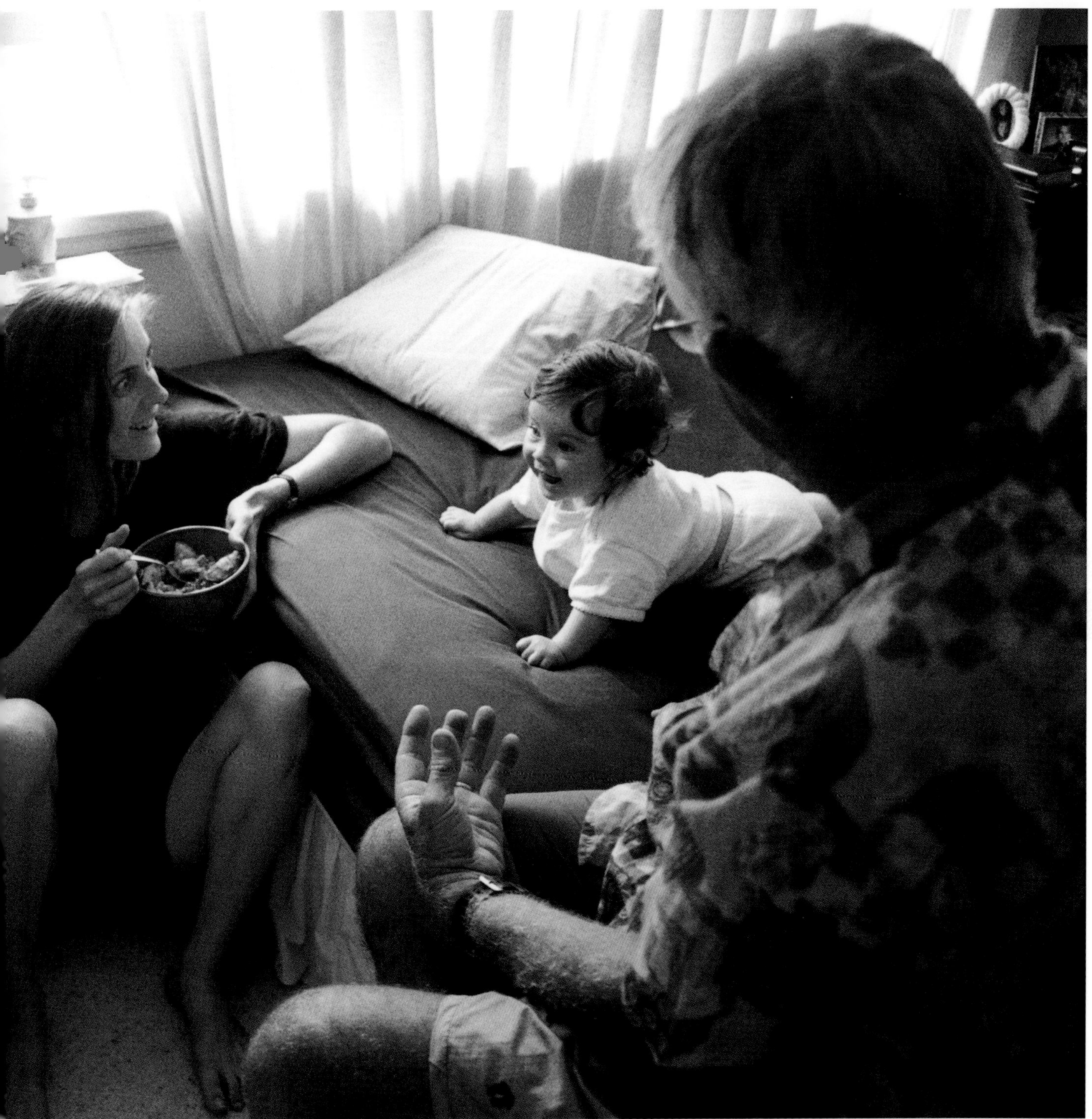

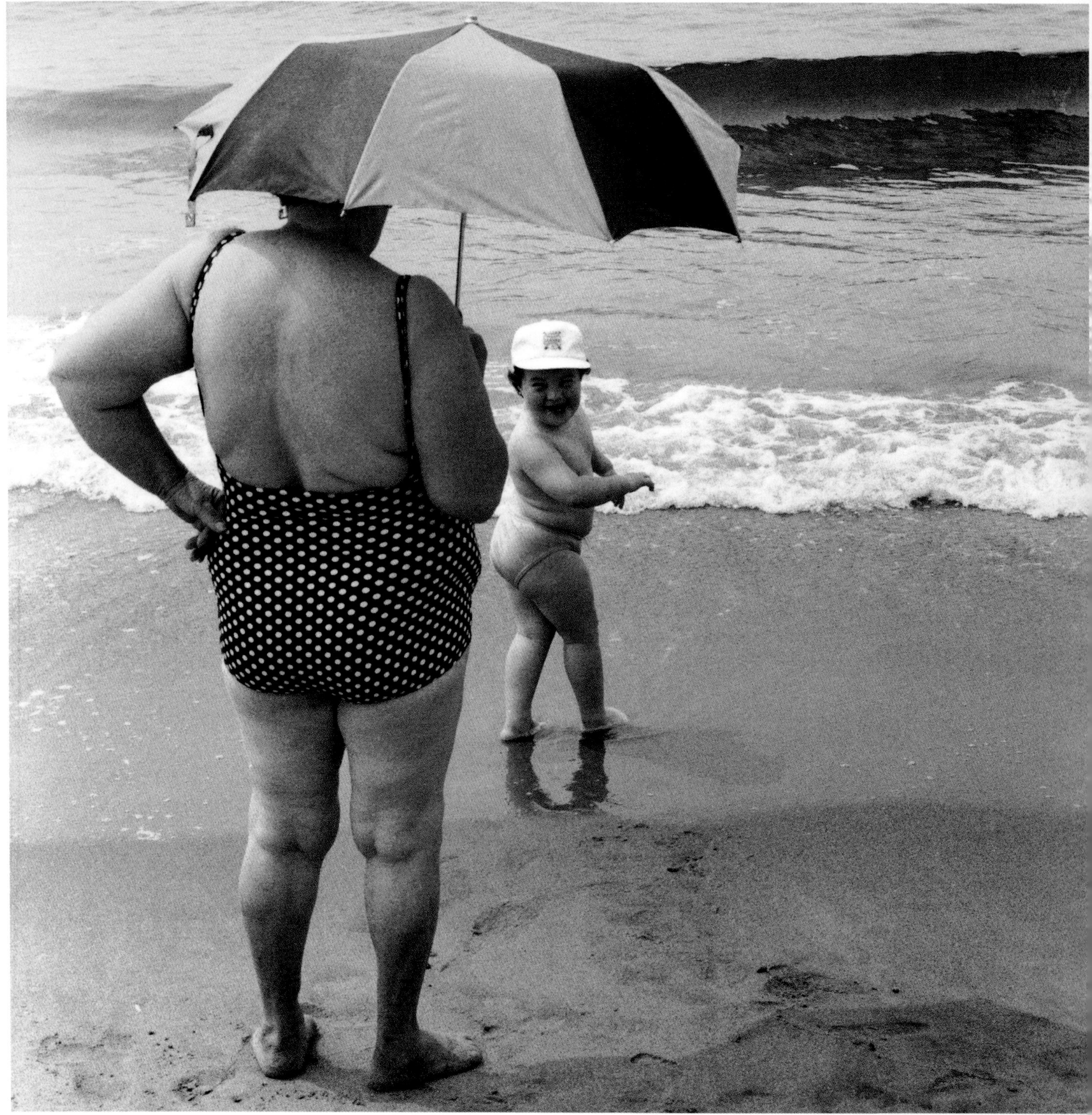

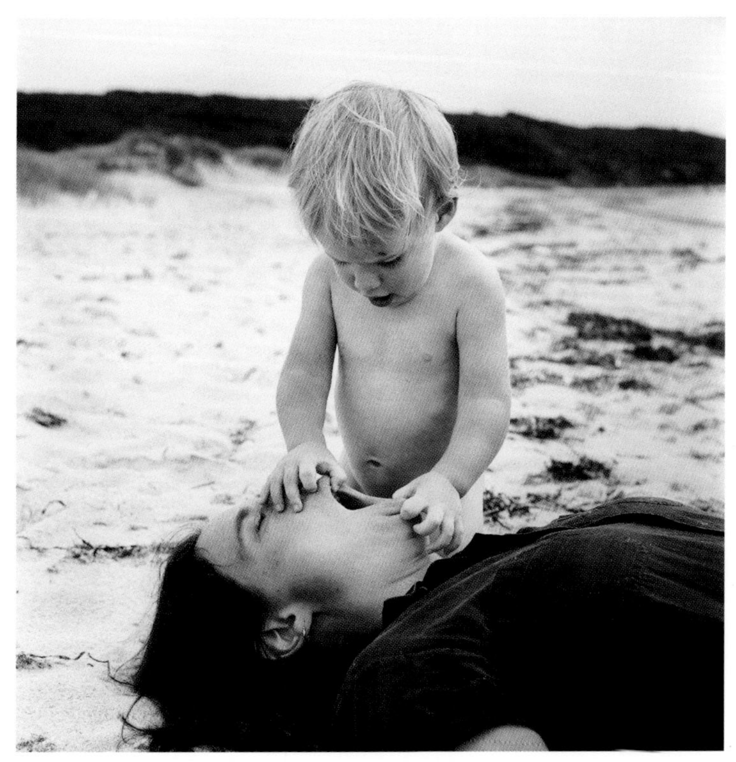

Joy is not in things, it is in us.

[RICHARD WAGNER]

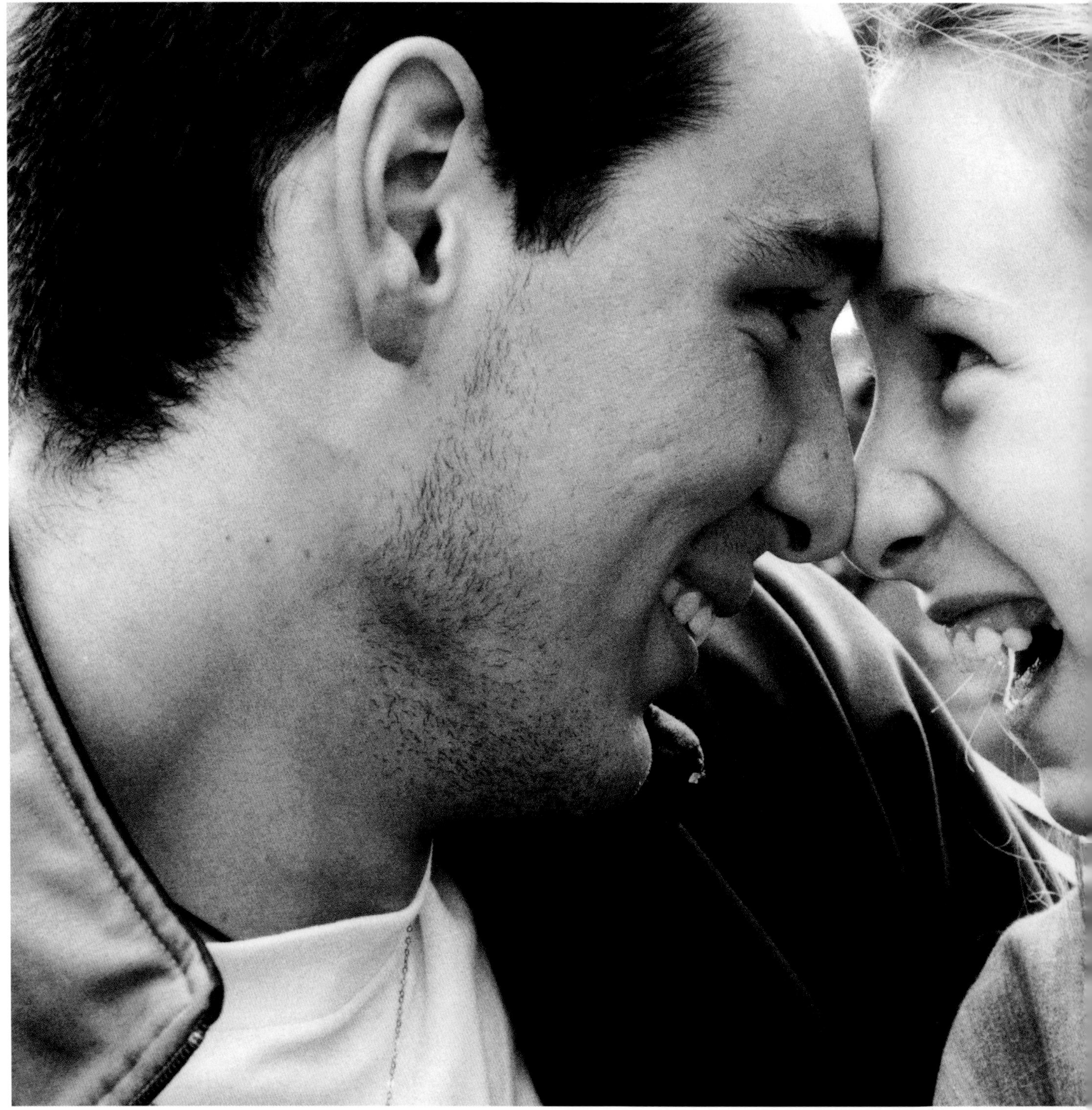

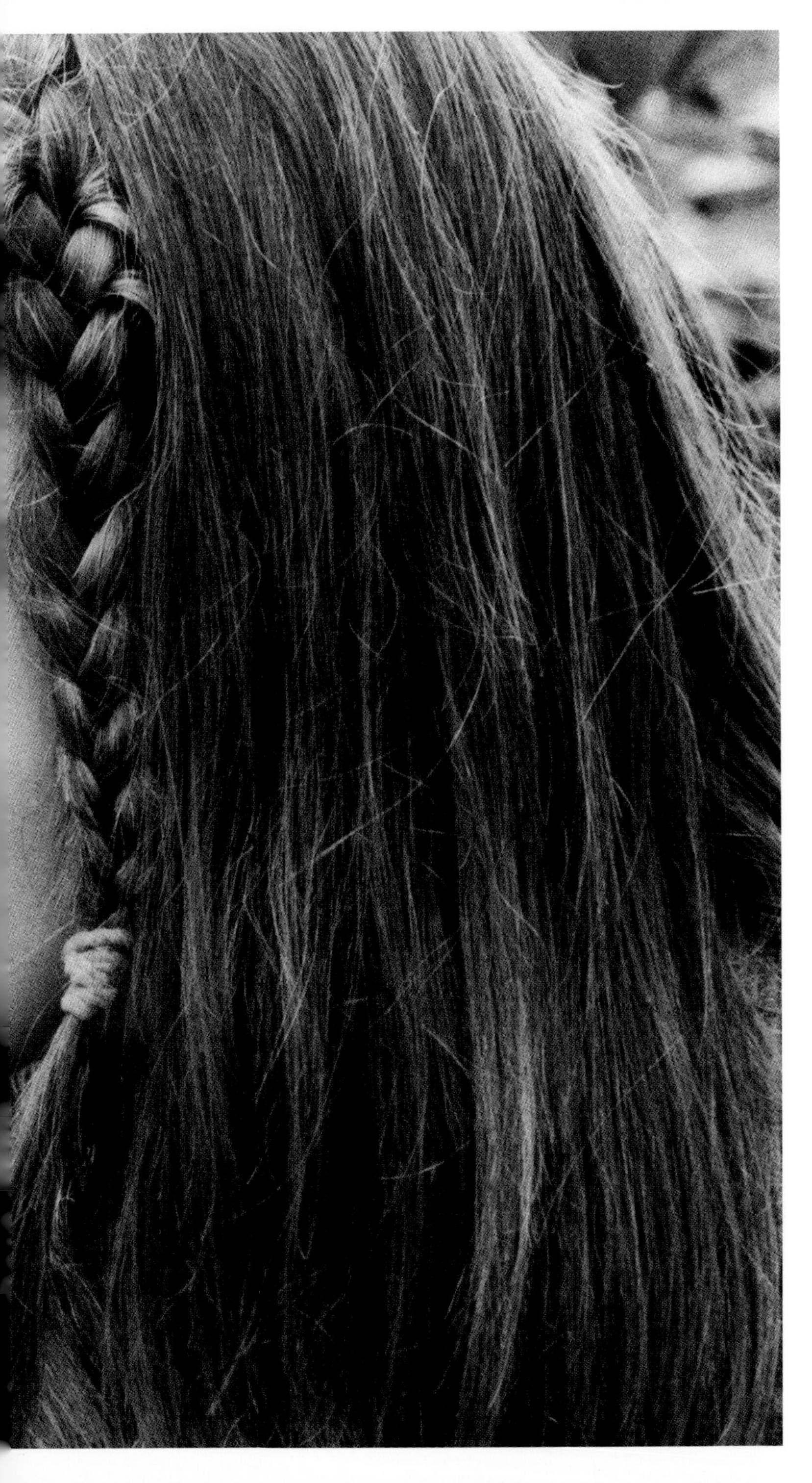

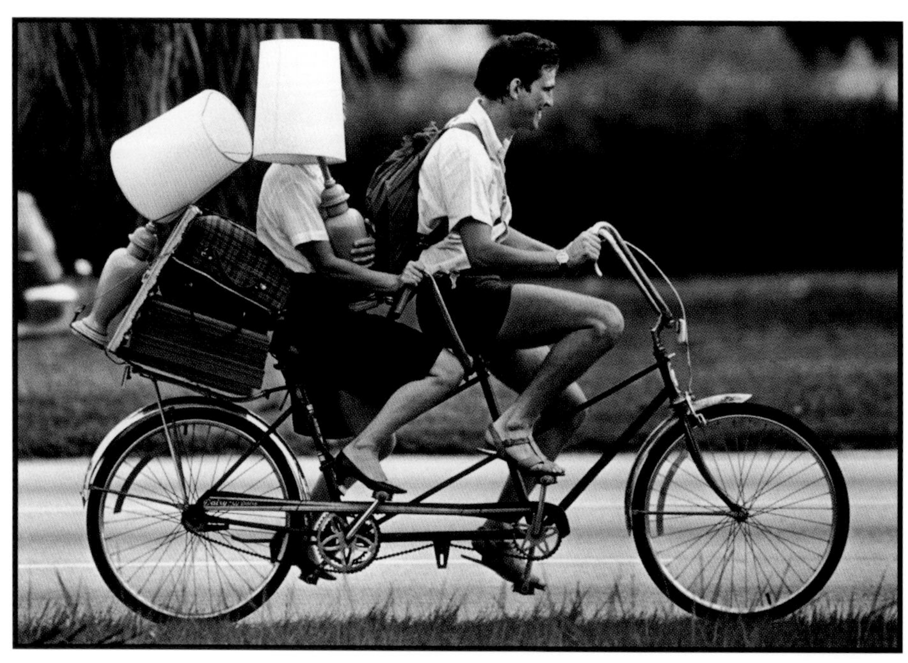

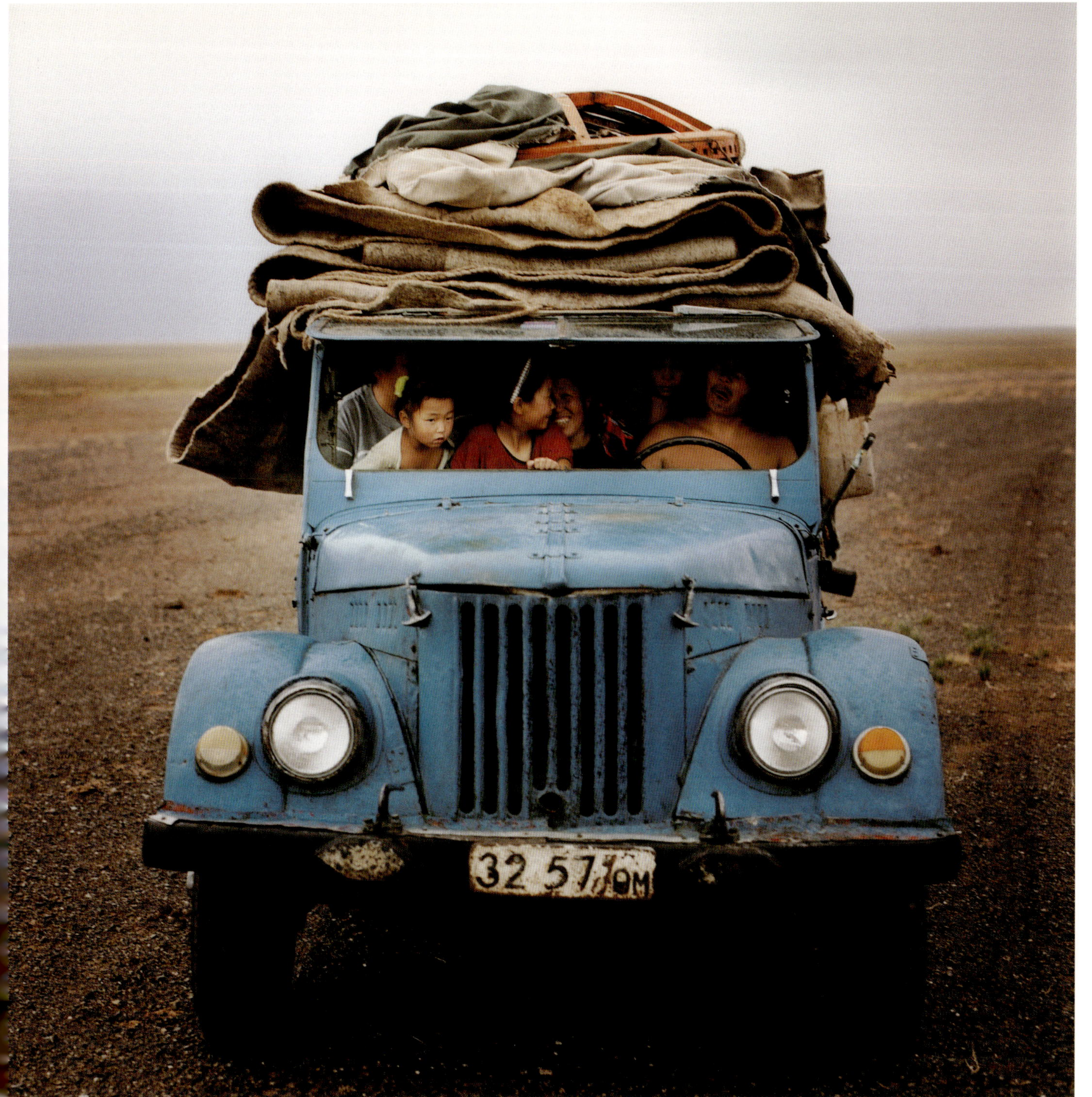
32 57 ОМ

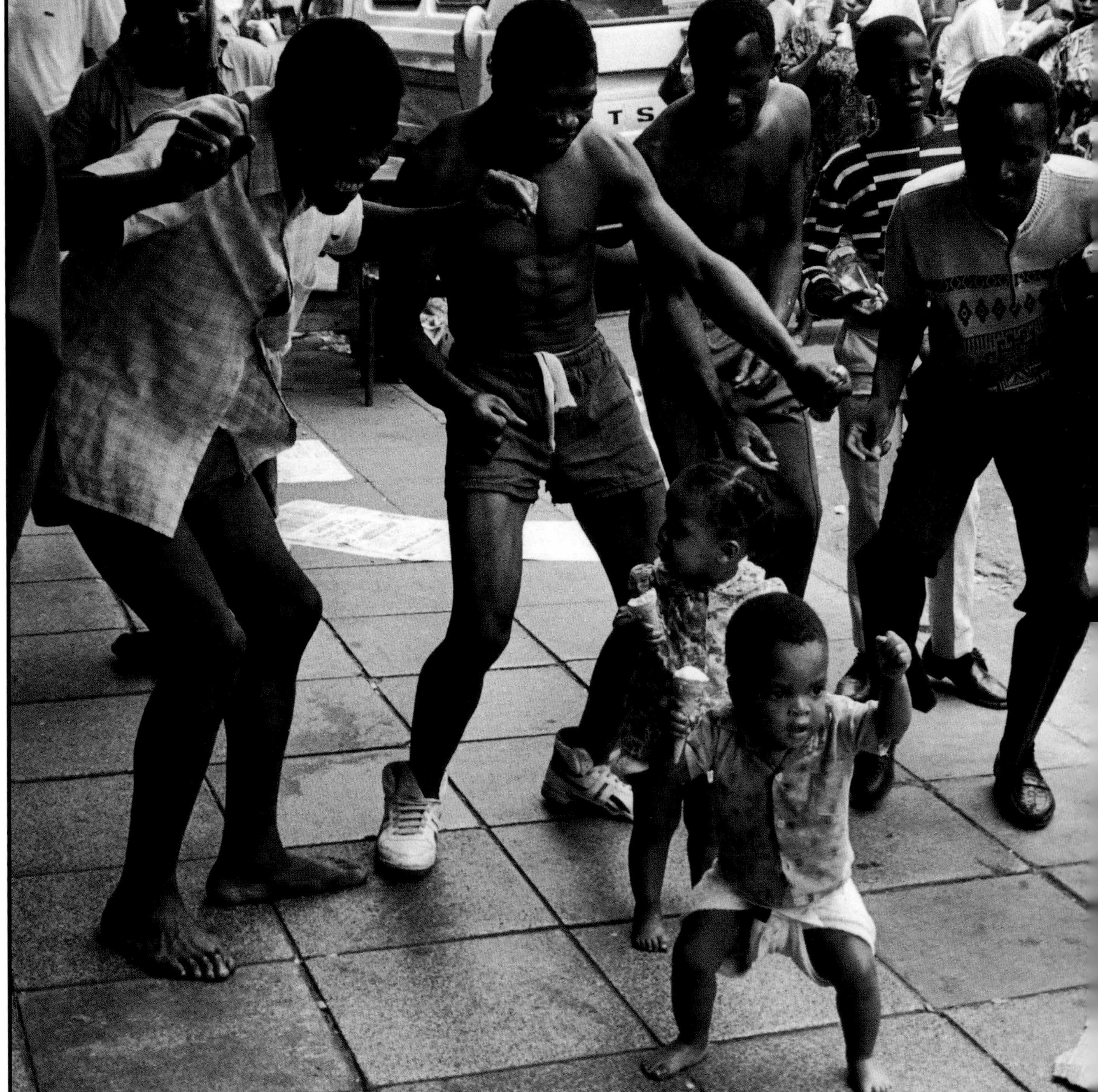

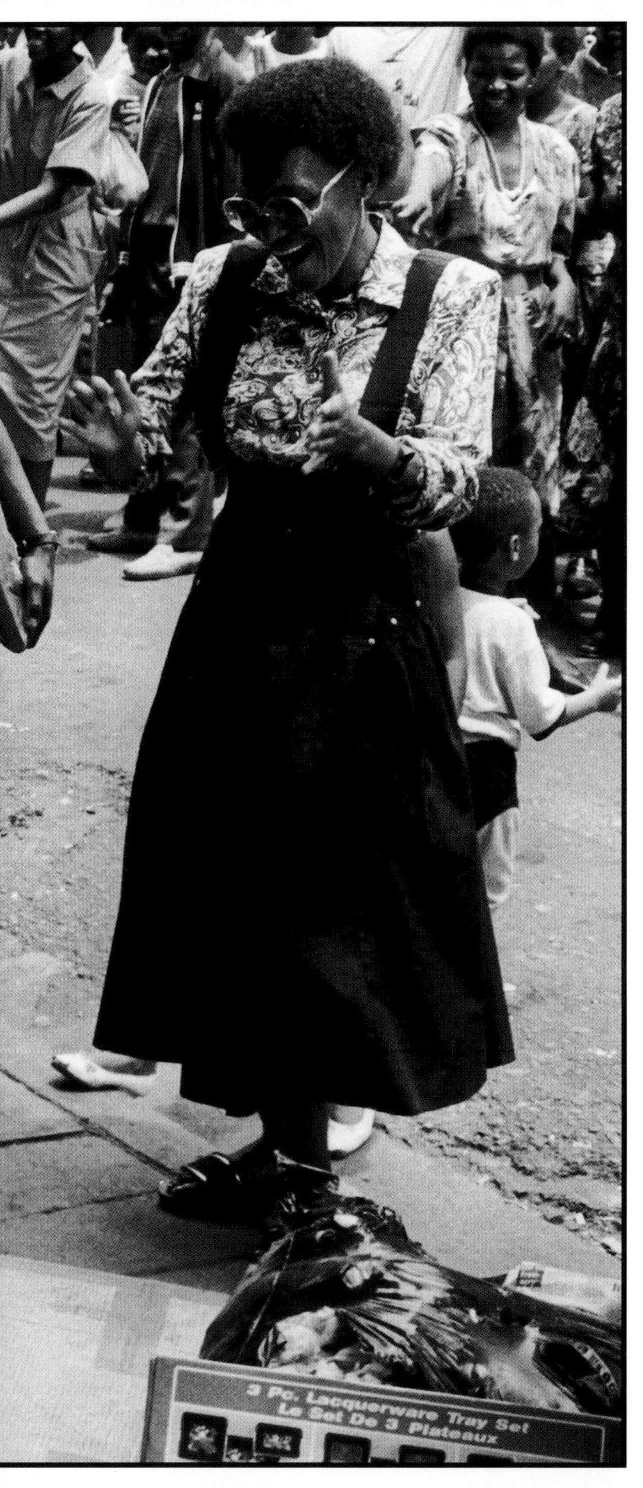
3 Pc. Lacquerware Tray Set
Le Set De 3 Plateaux

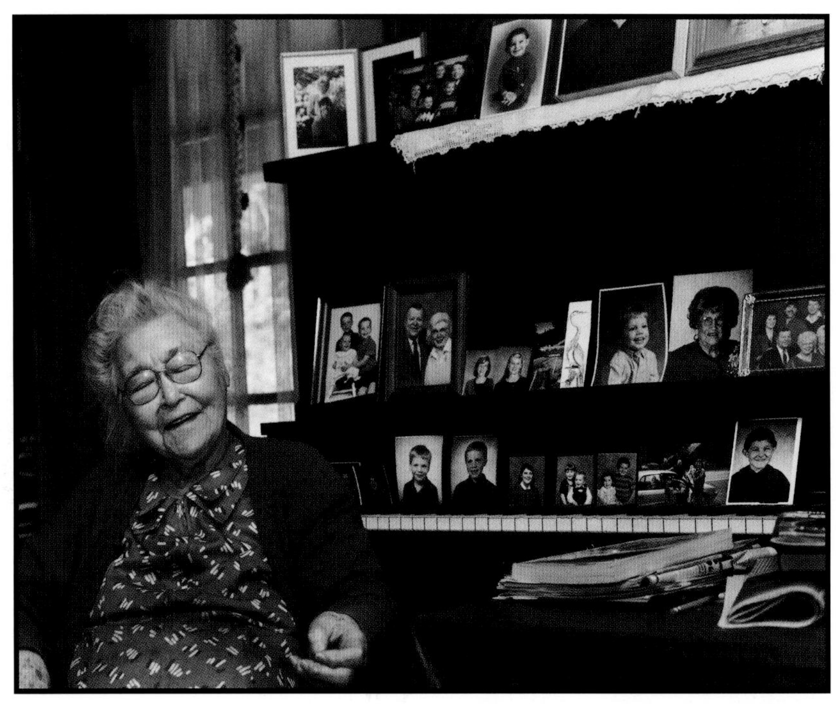

I live for those who love me,
for those who **know** me true.

[GEORGE LINNAEUS BANKS]

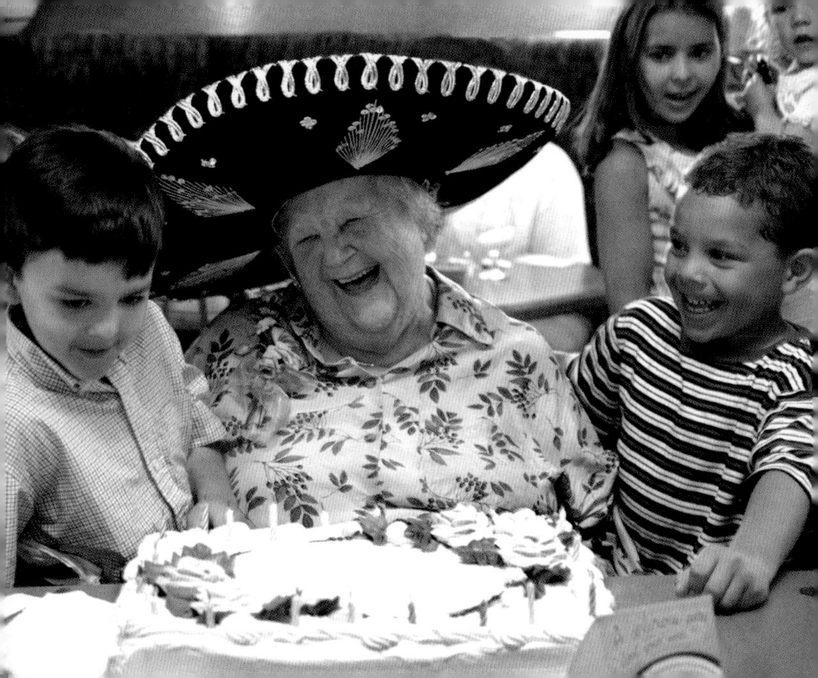

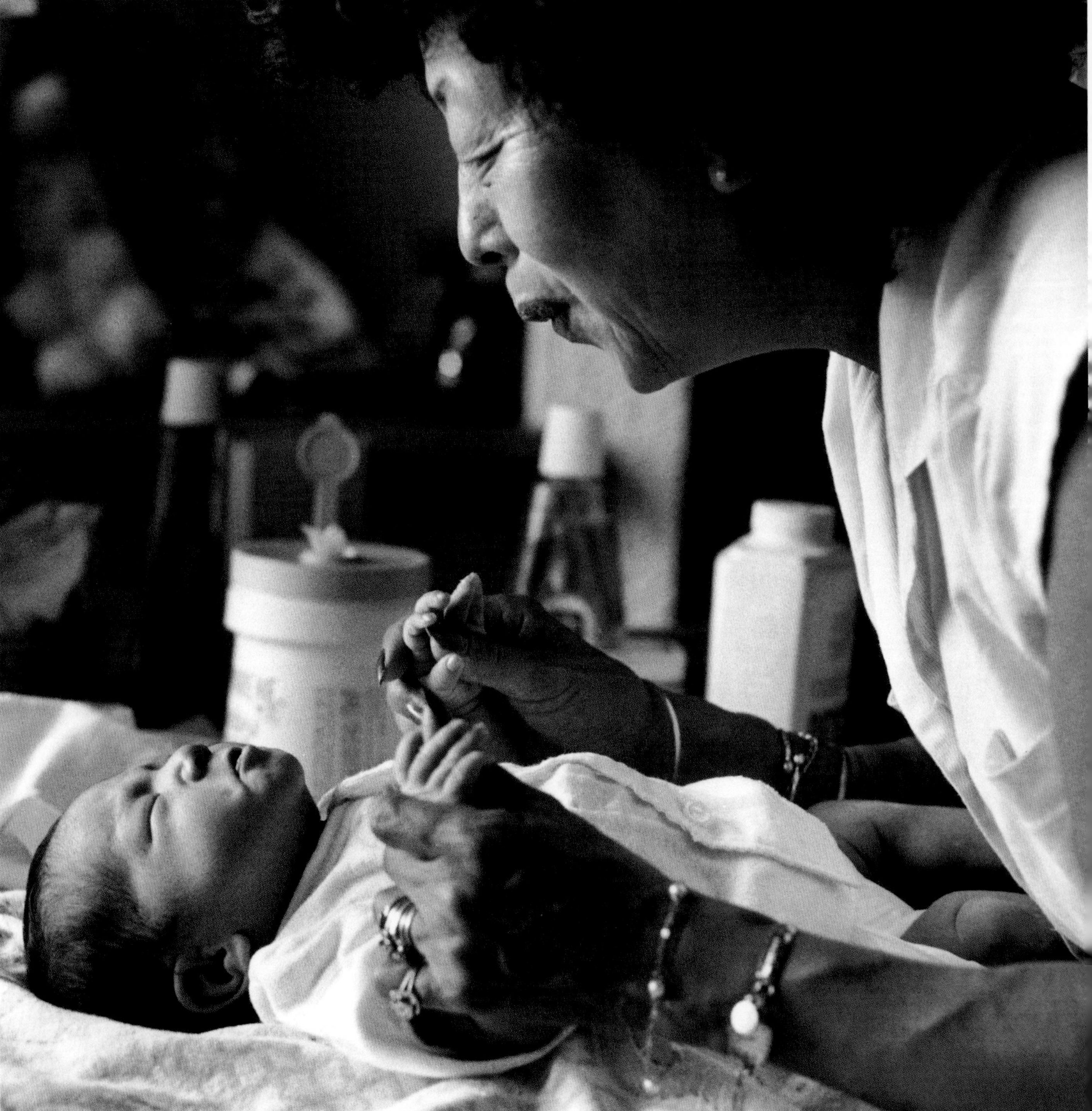

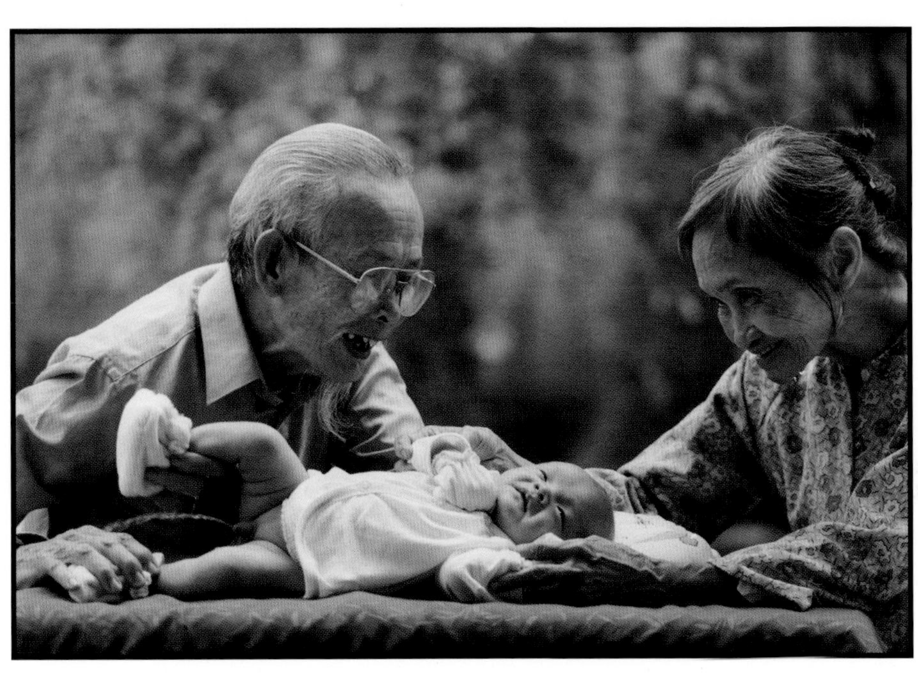

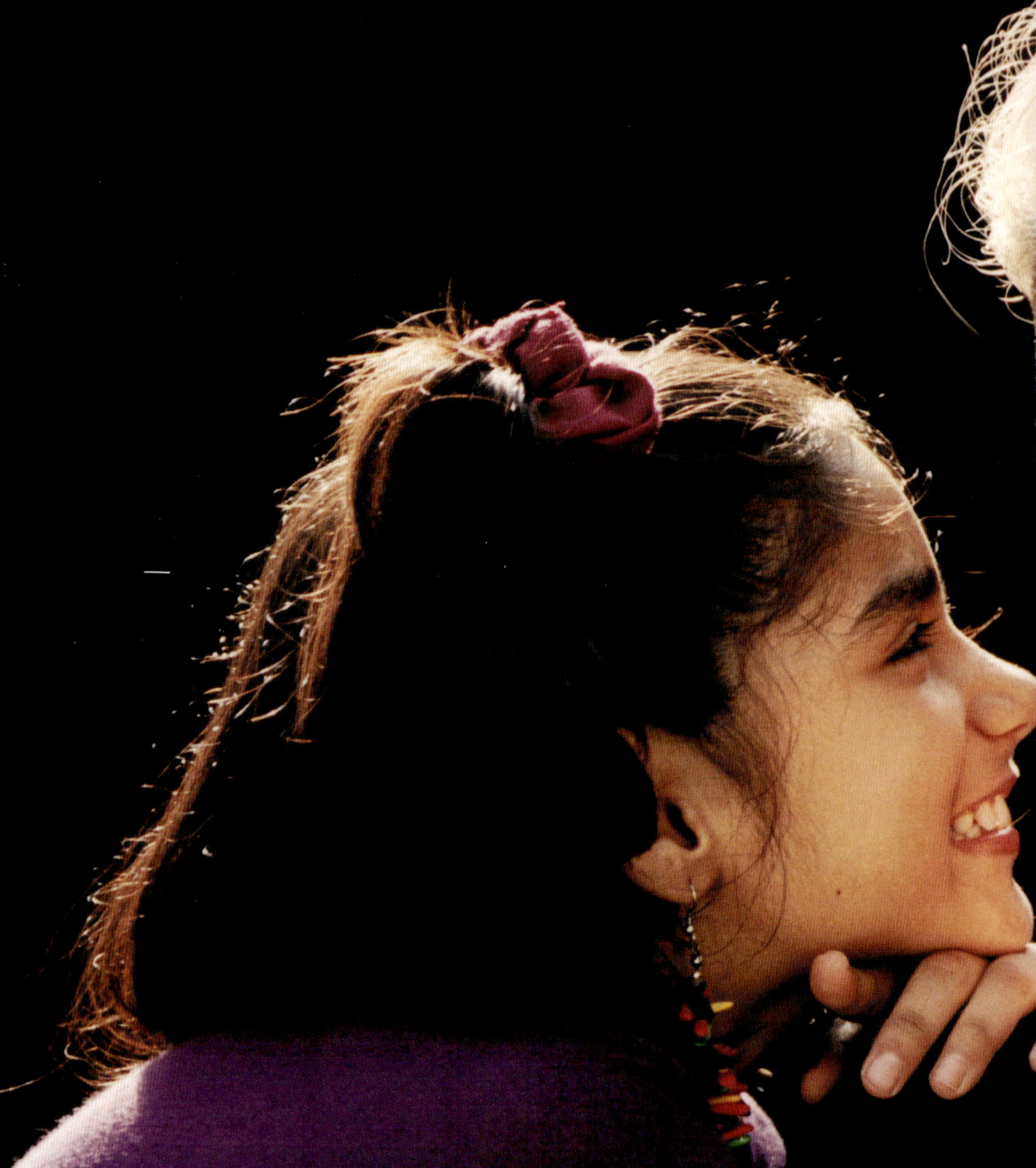

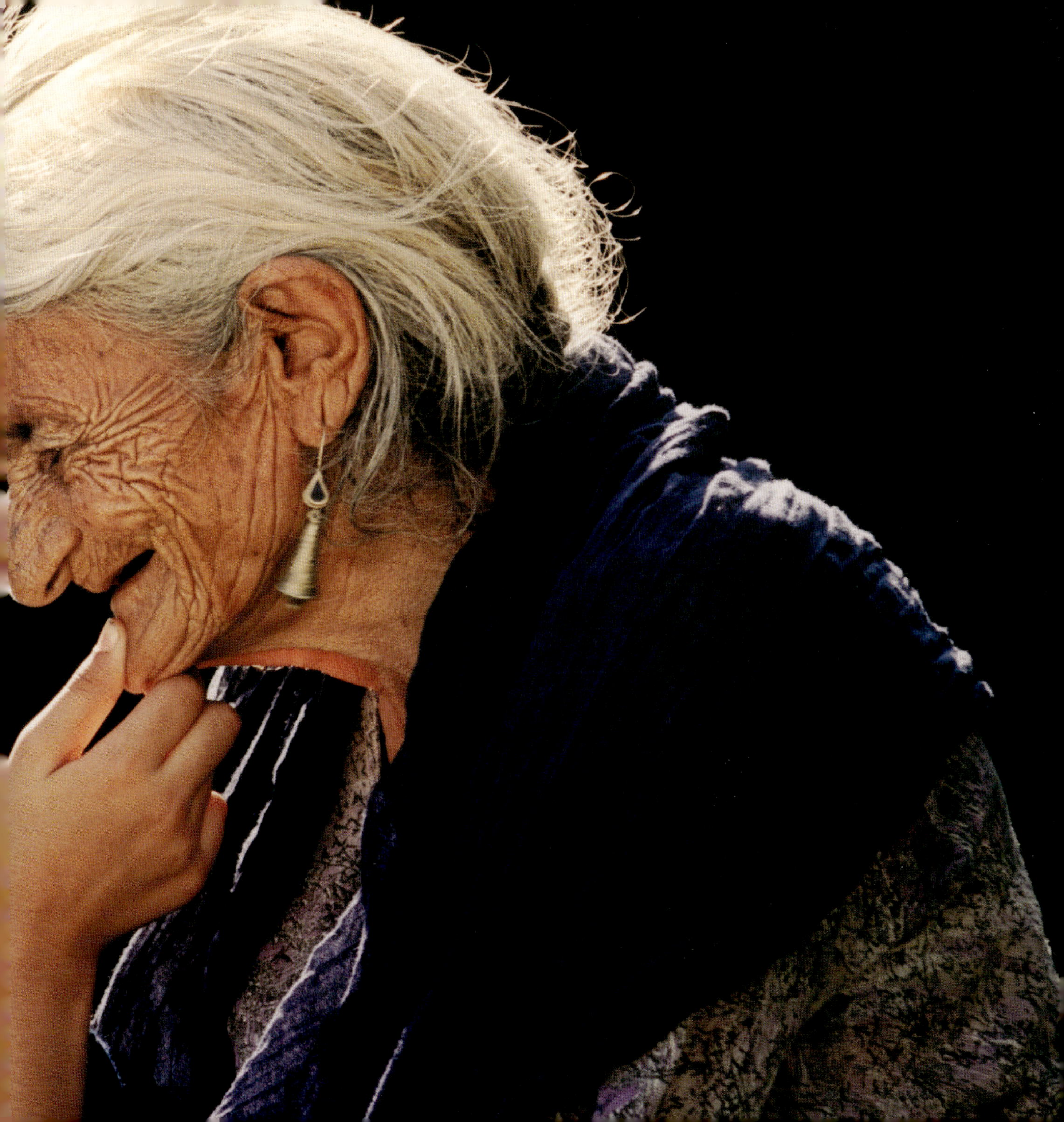

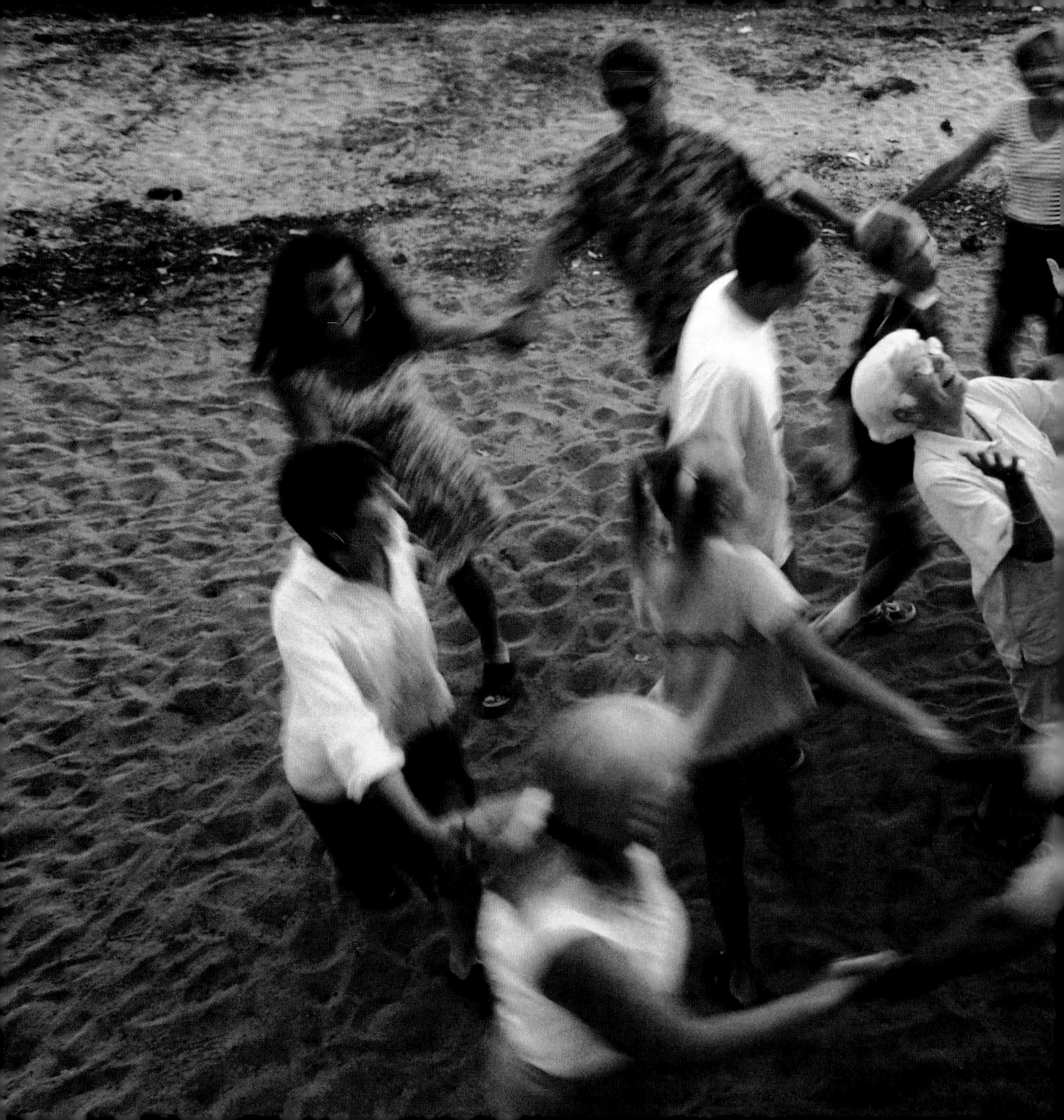

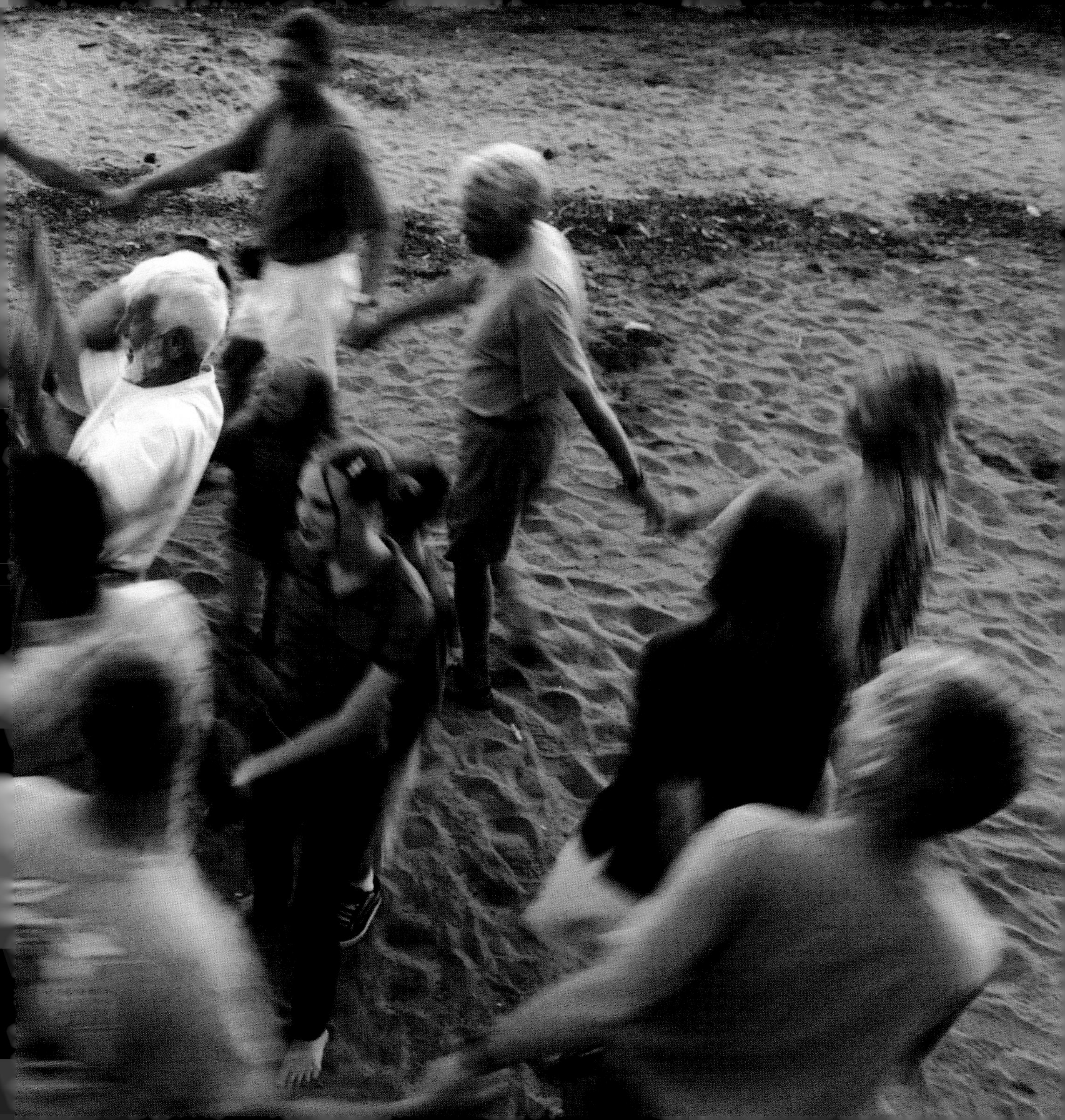

Laughter is the shortest distance between

two people.

[VICTOR BORGE]

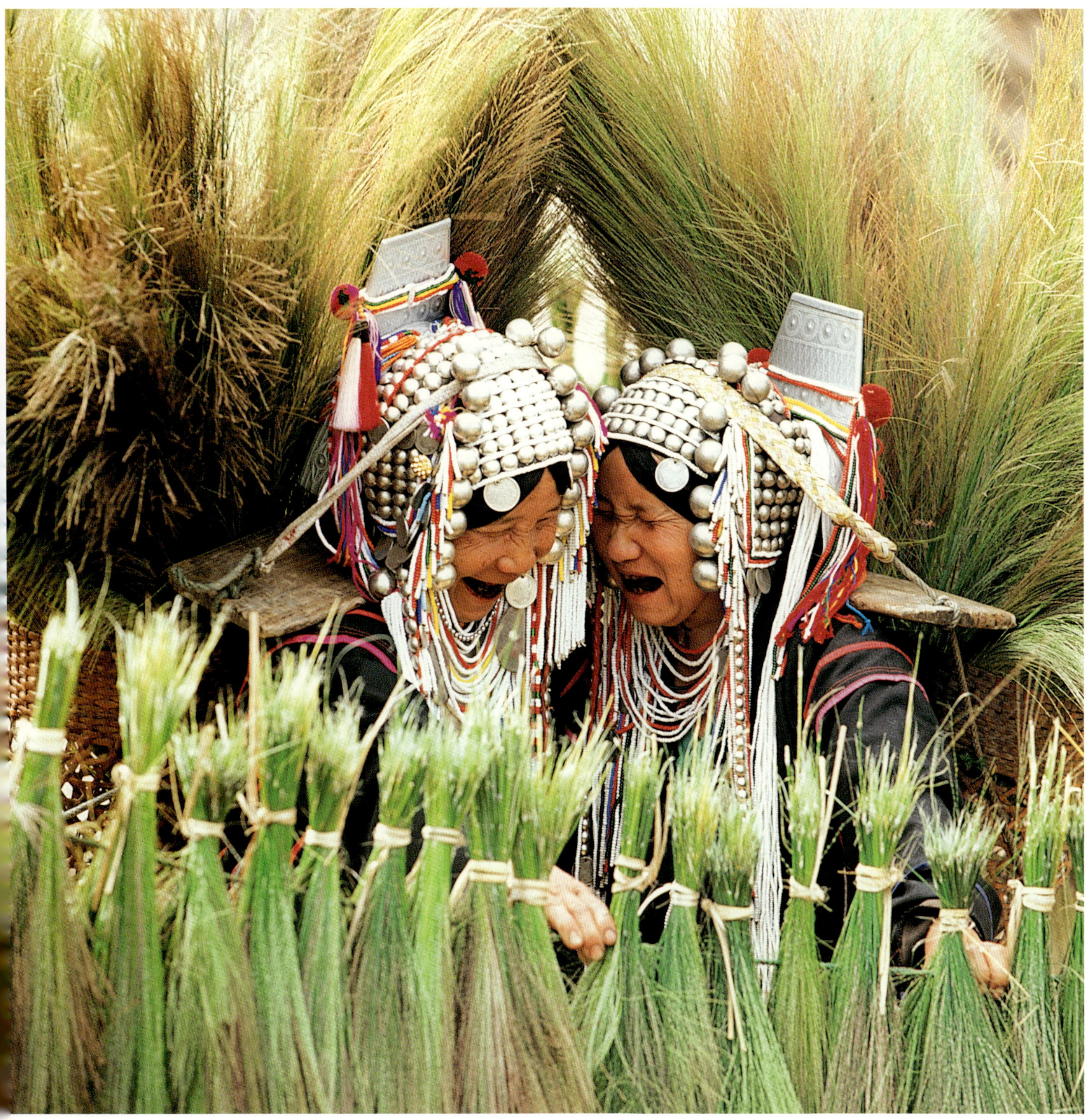

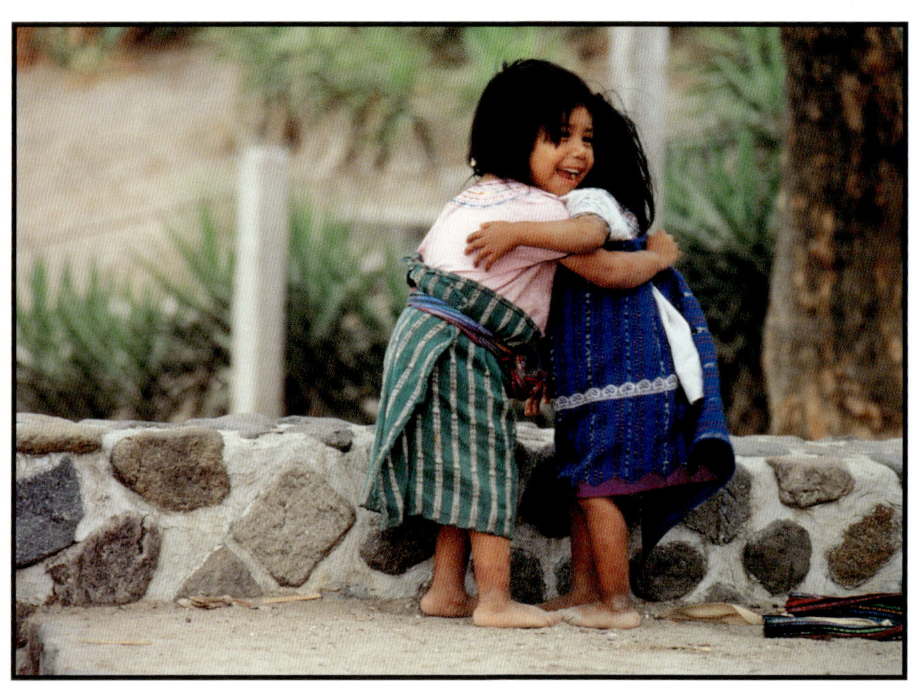

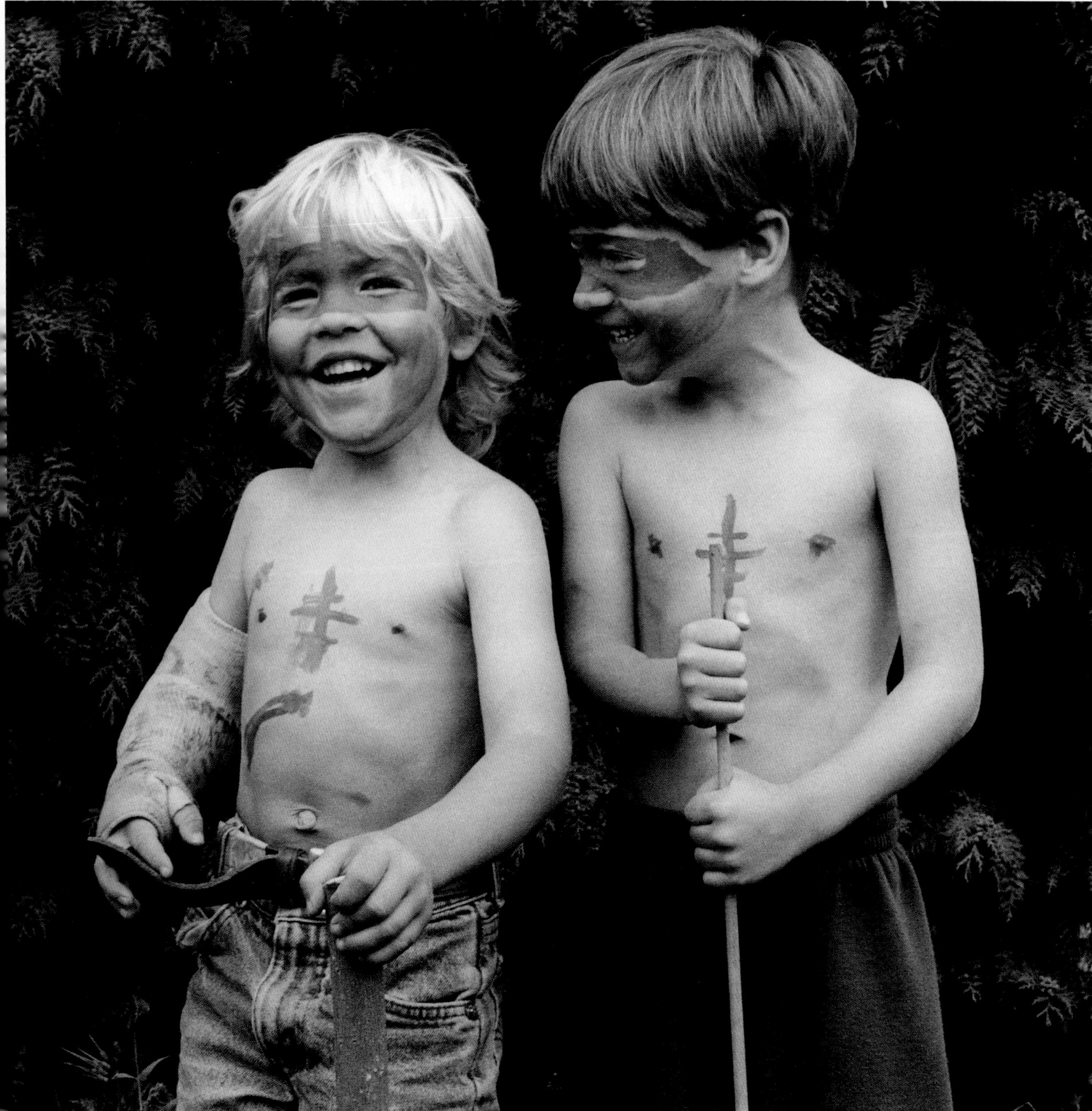

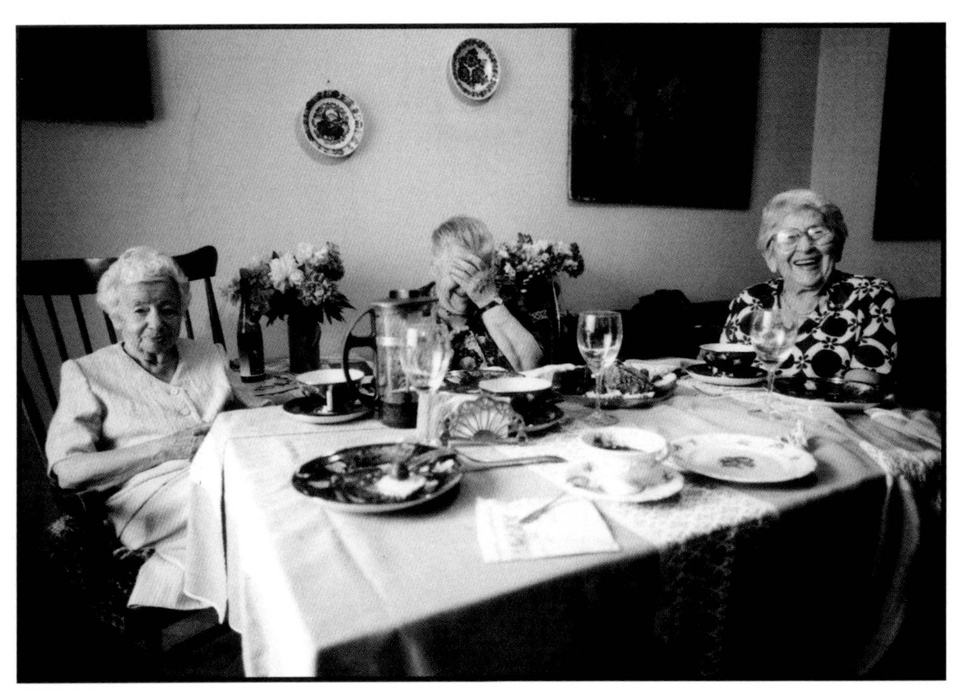

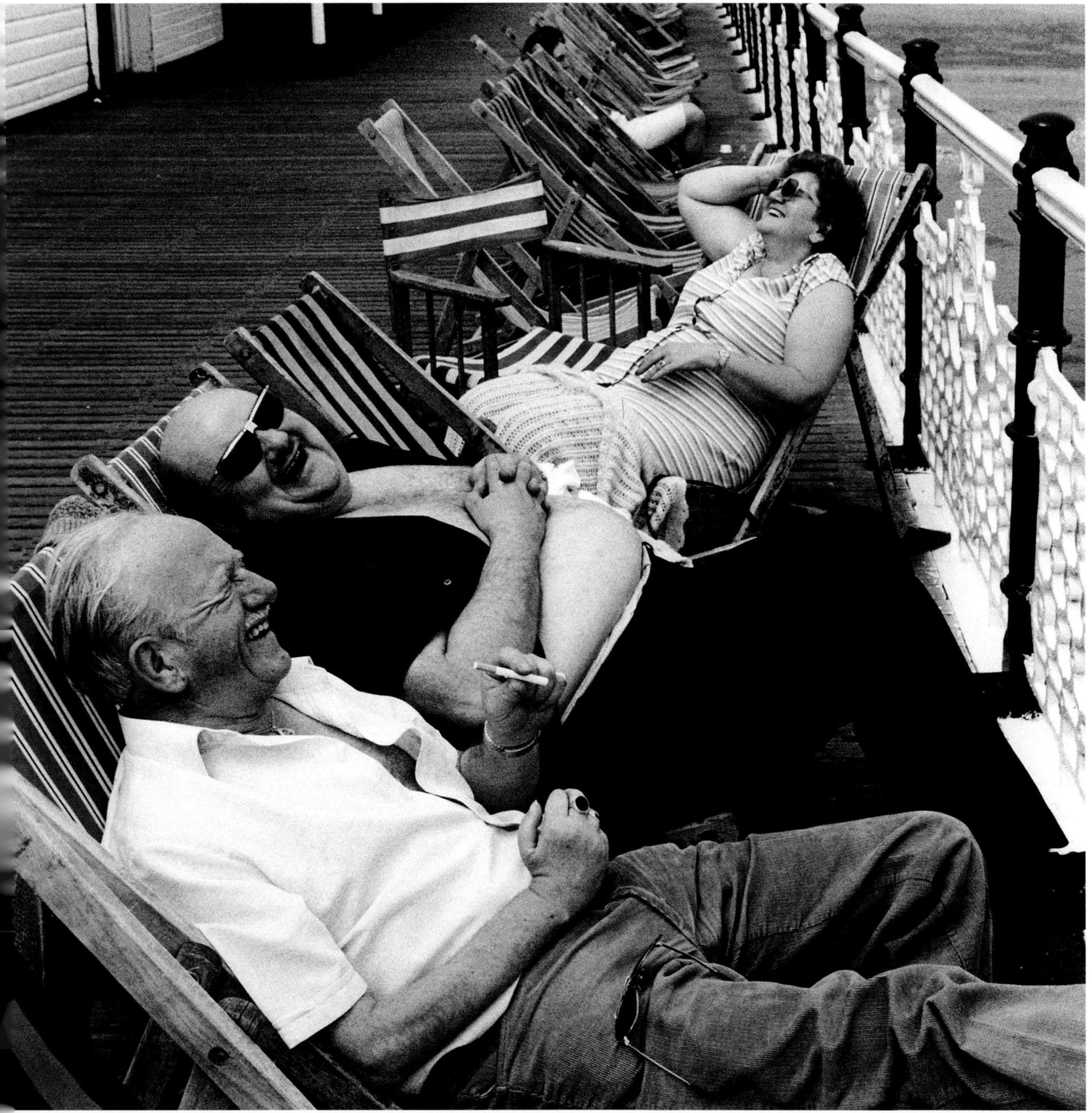

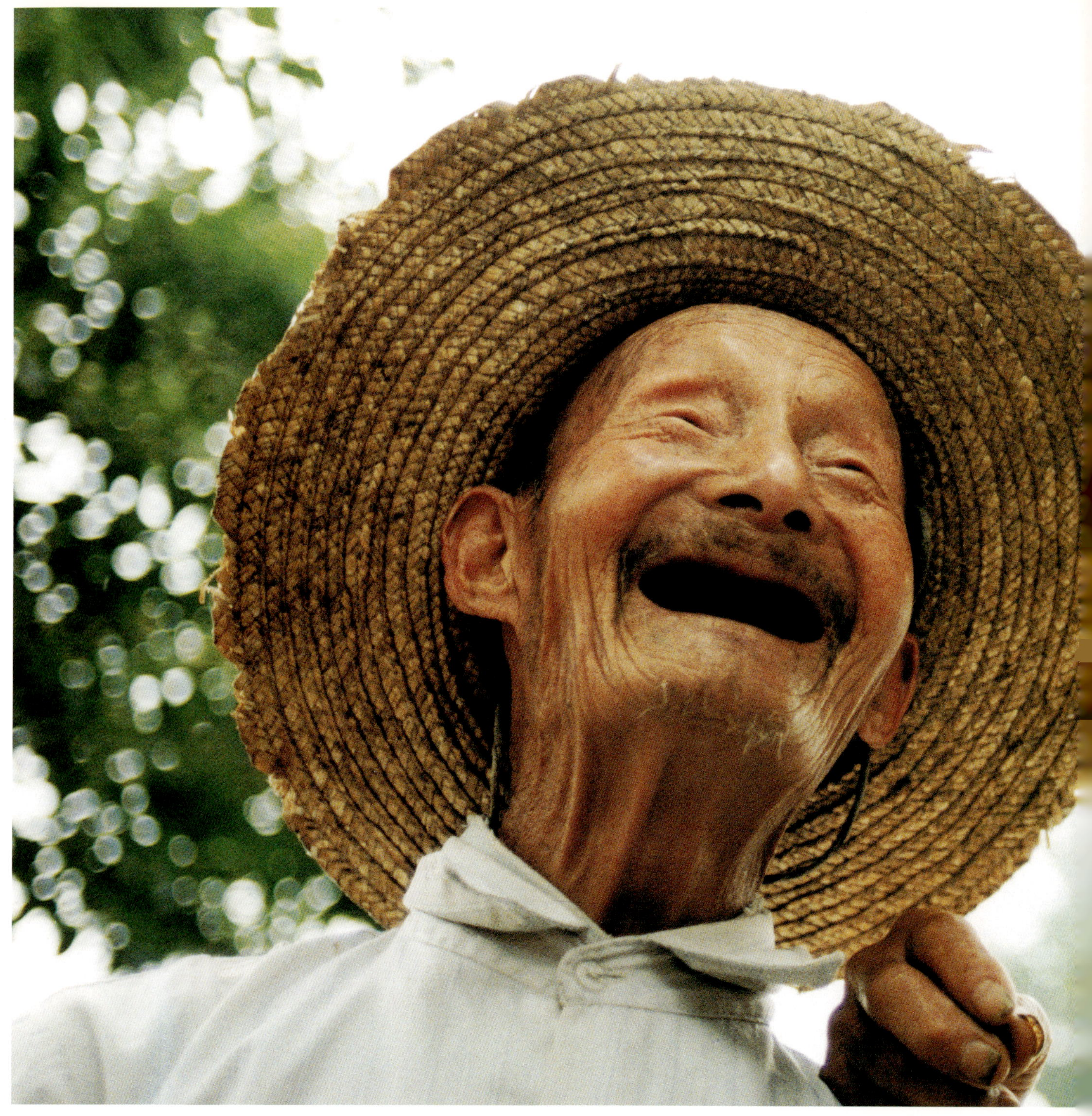

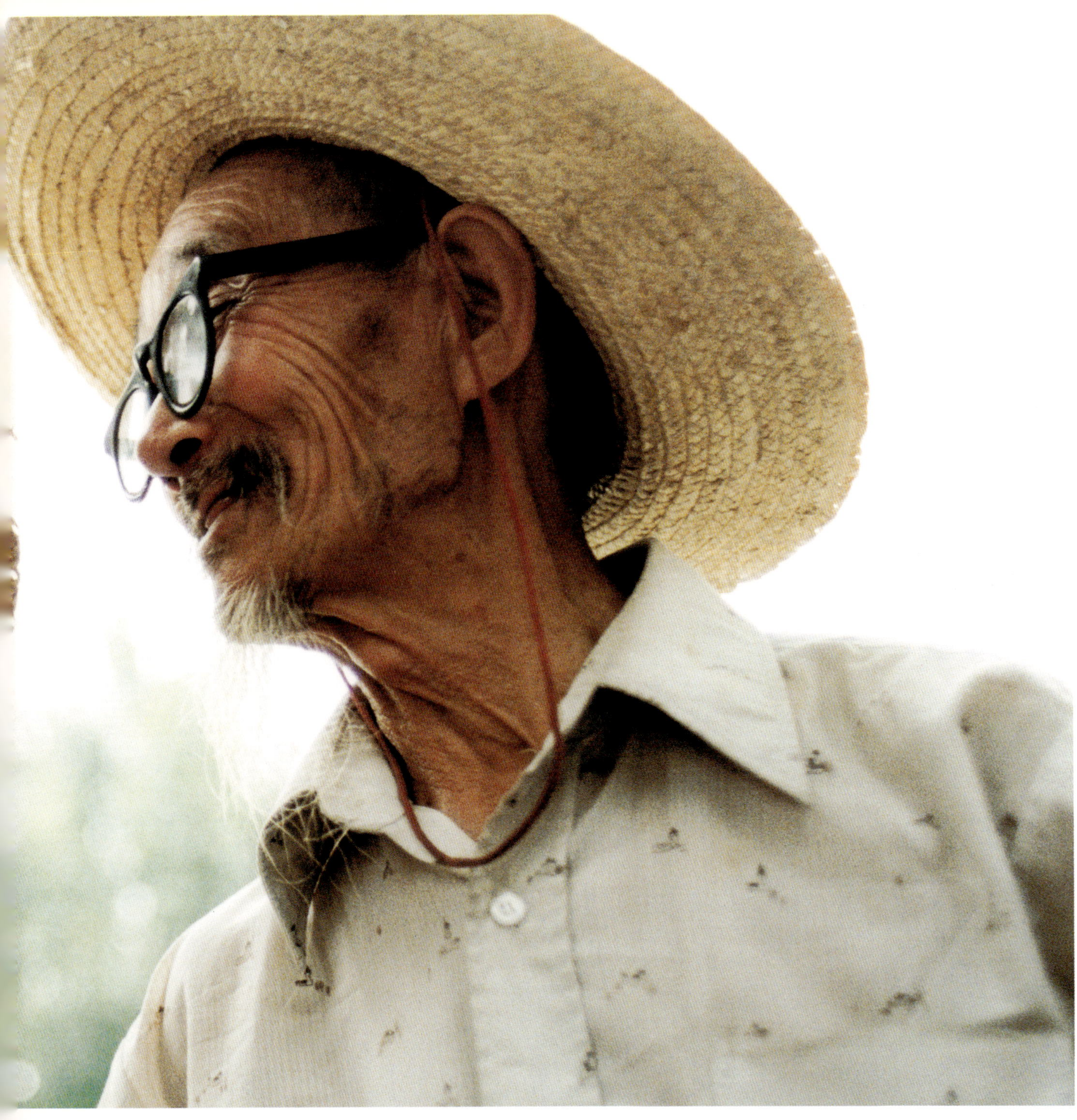

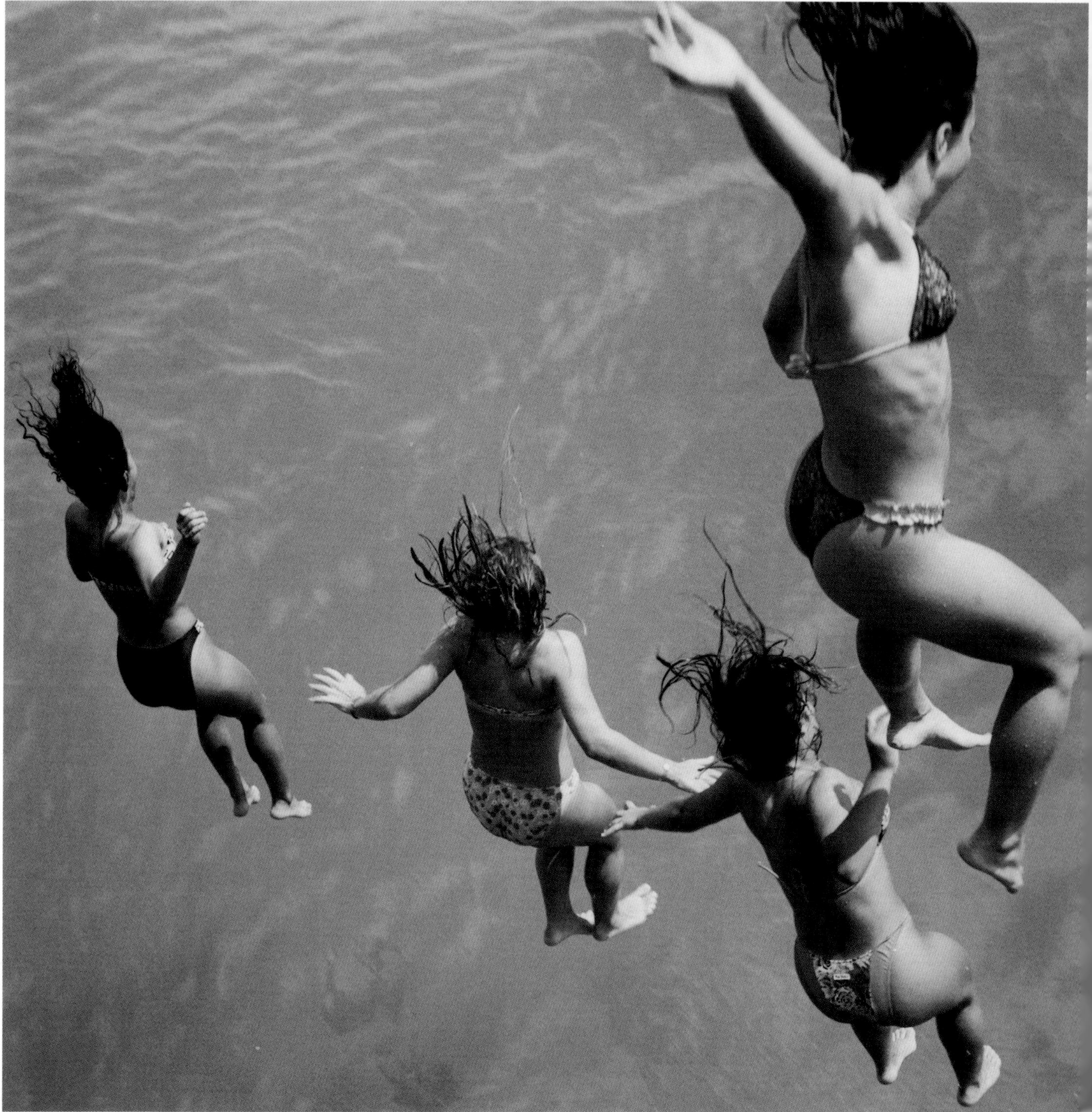

For memory has painted this perfect day, with colours that never fade...

[CARRIE JACOBS BOND]

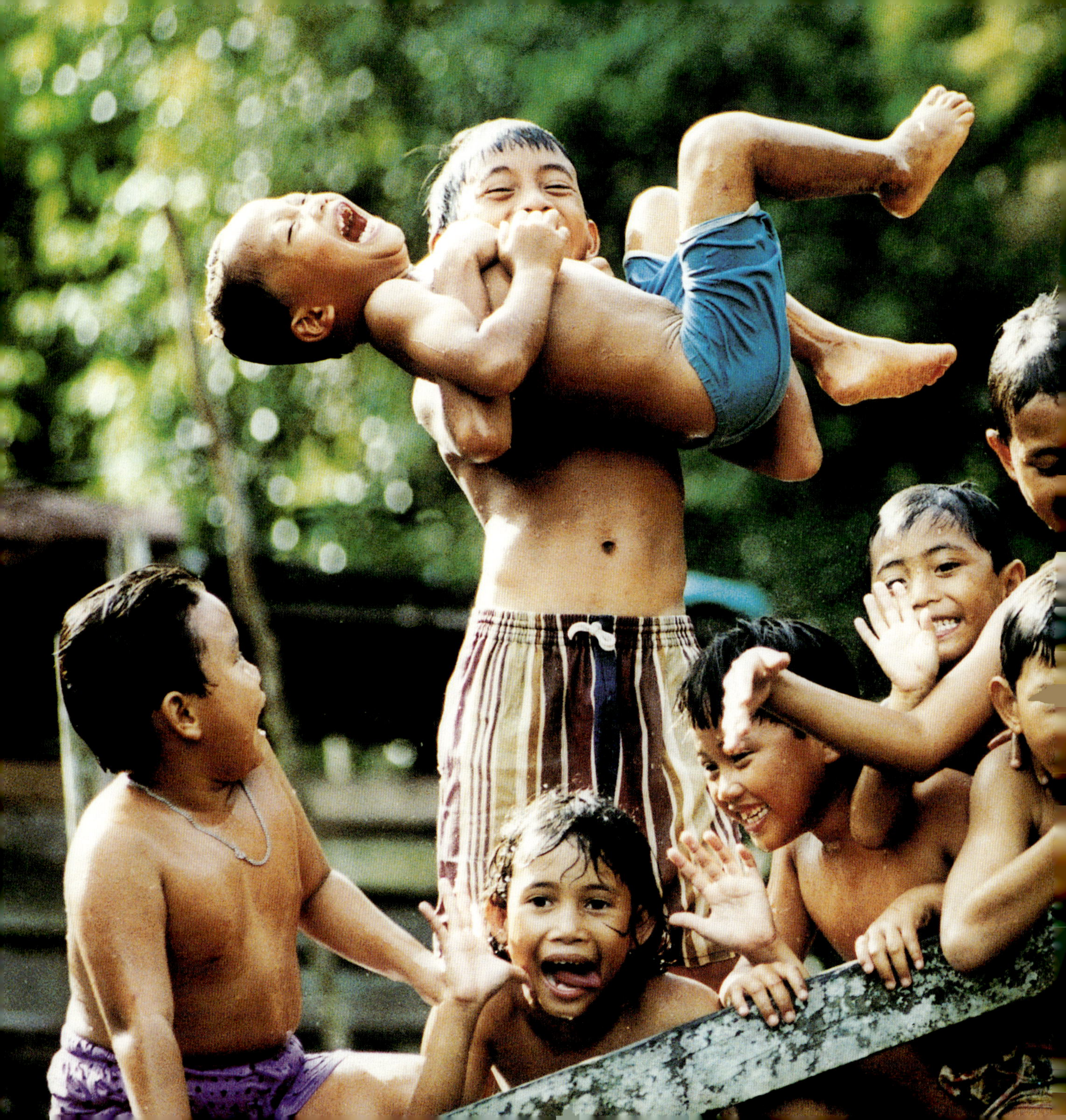

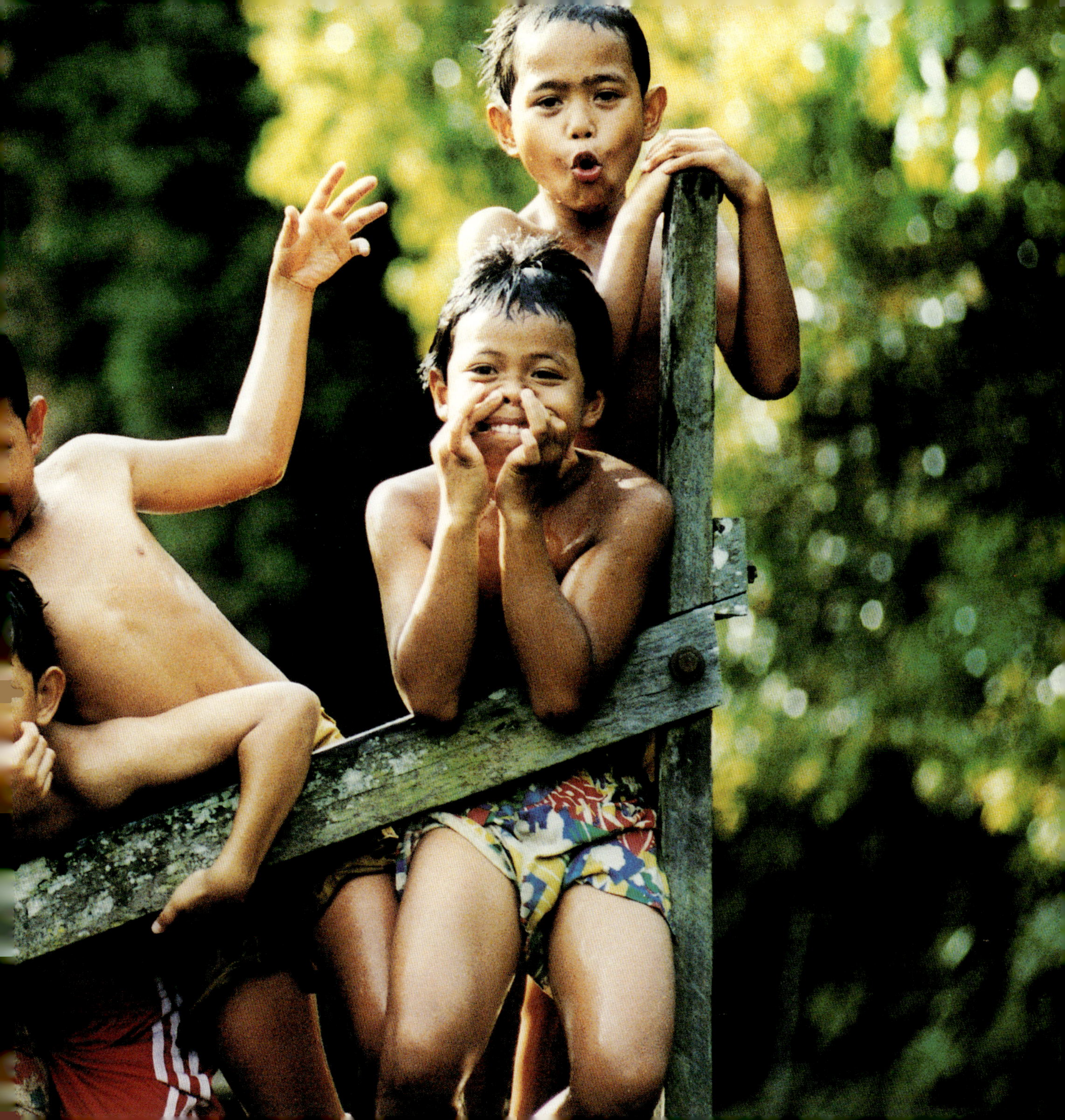

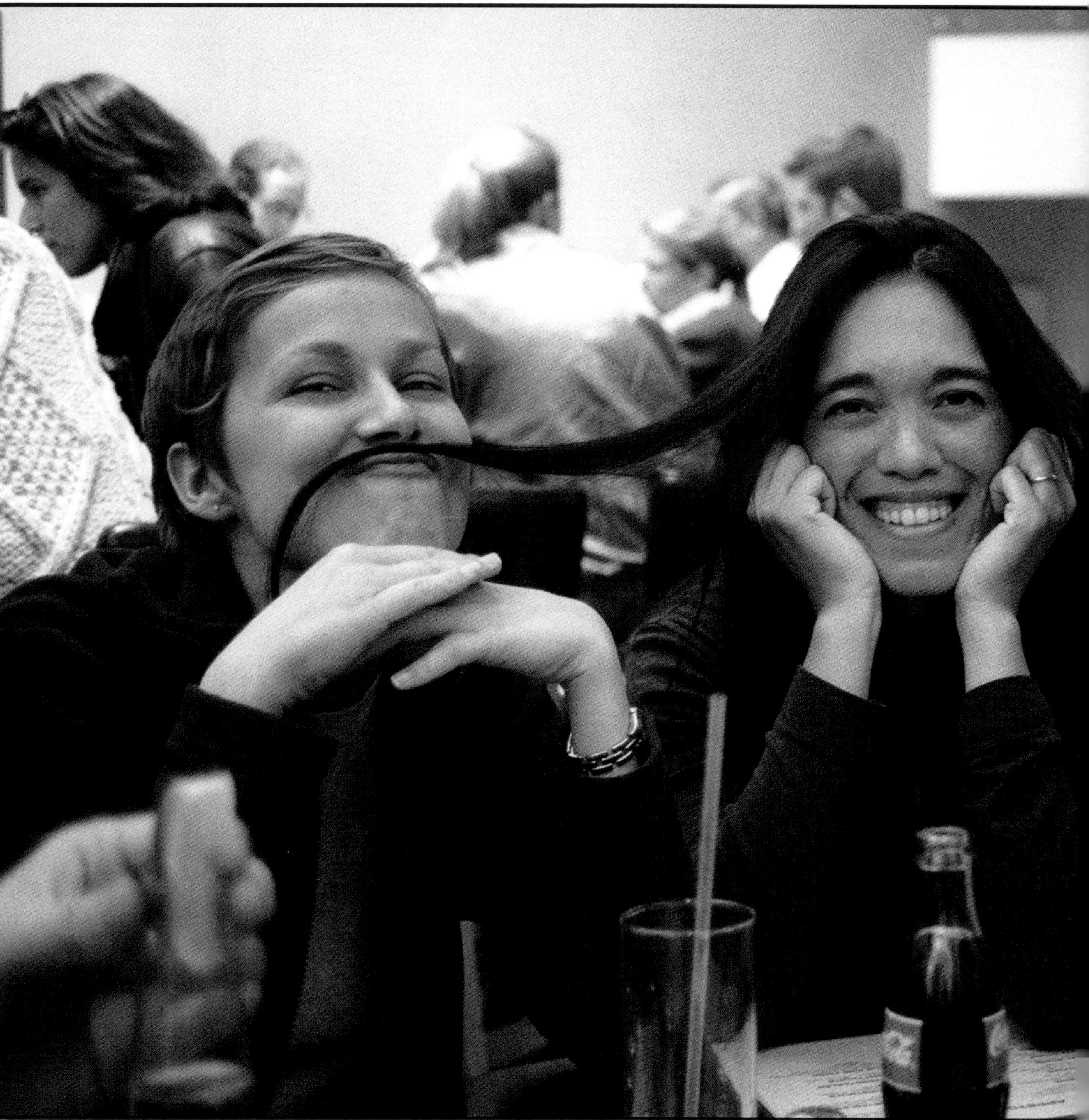

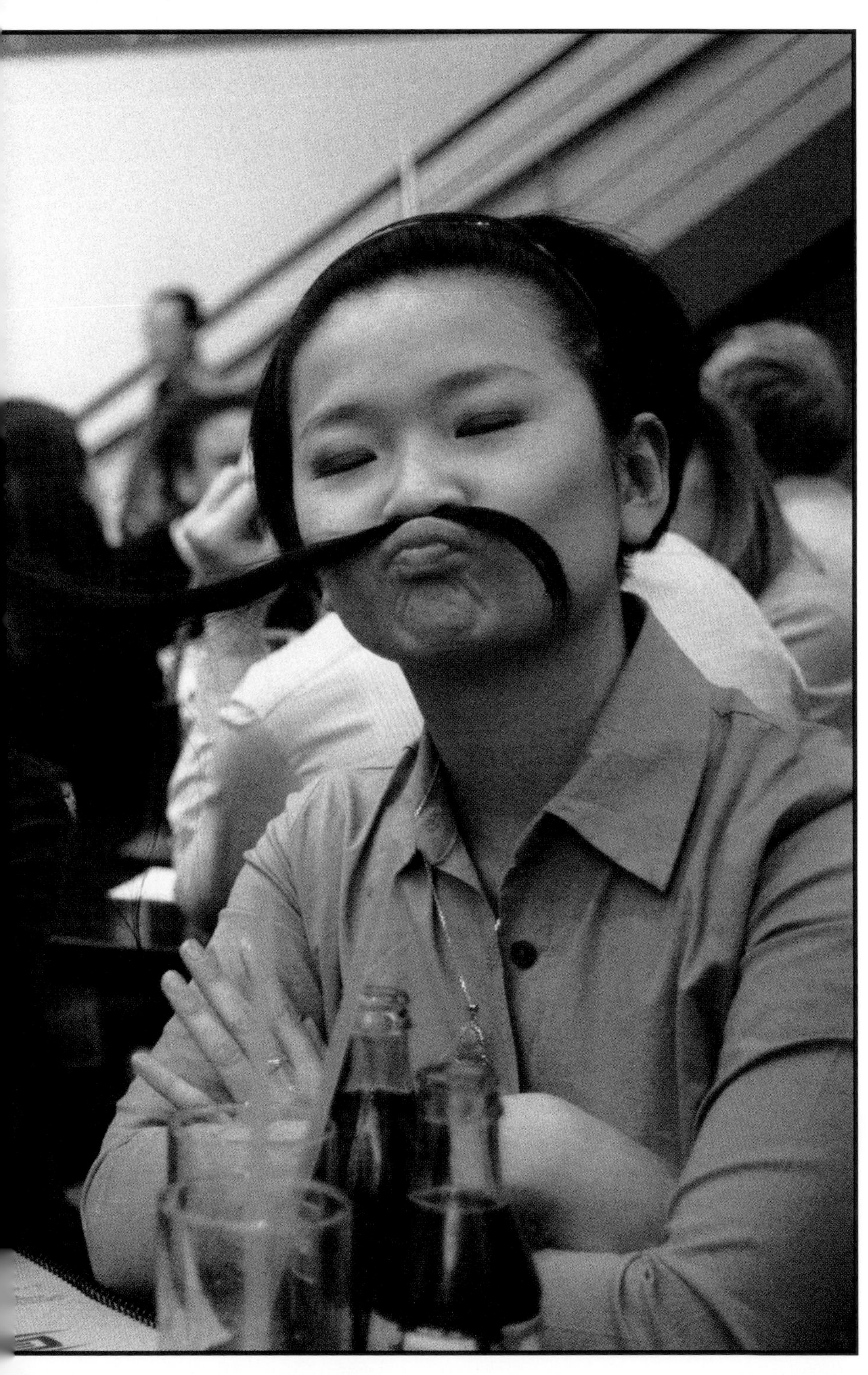

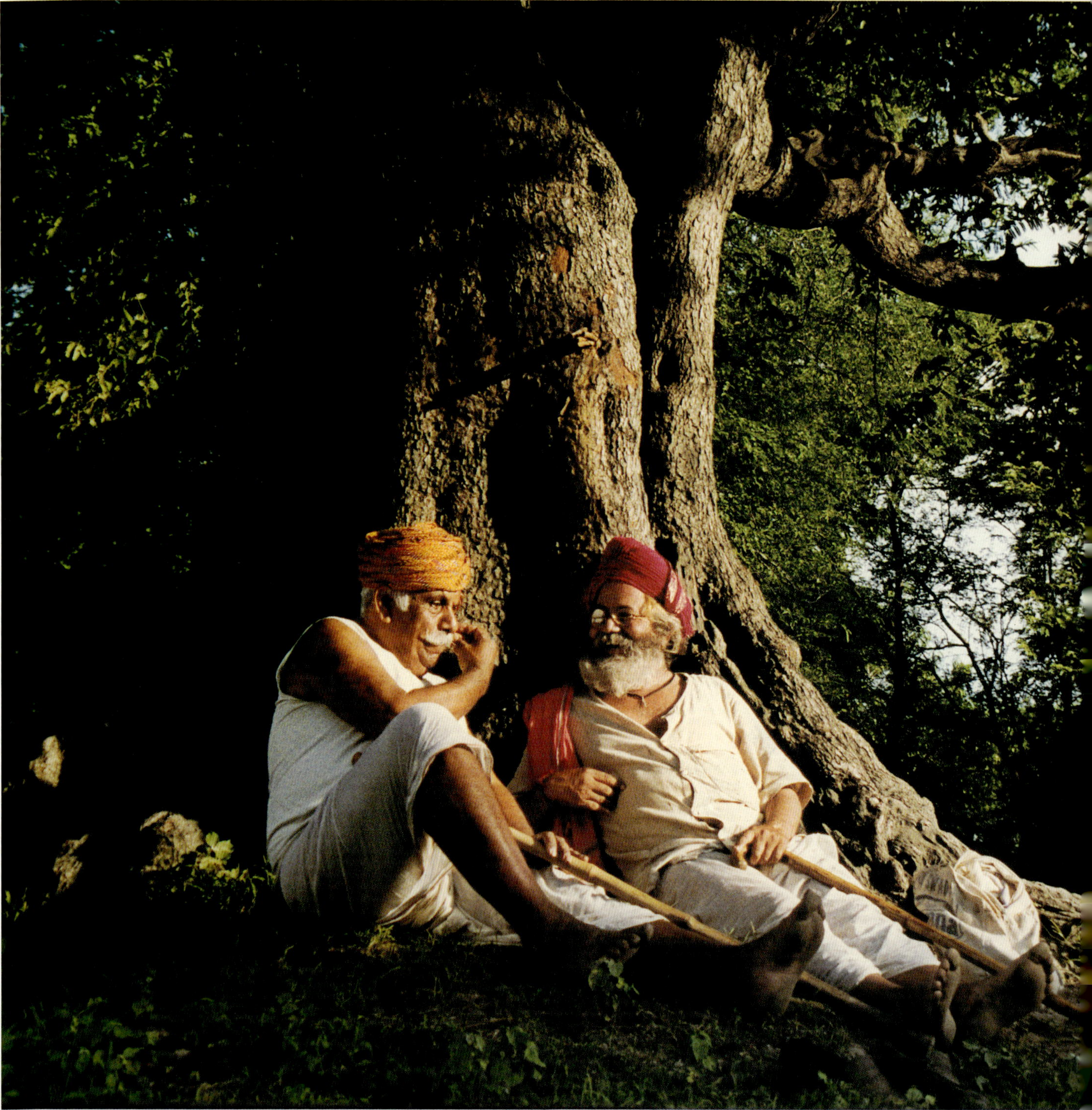

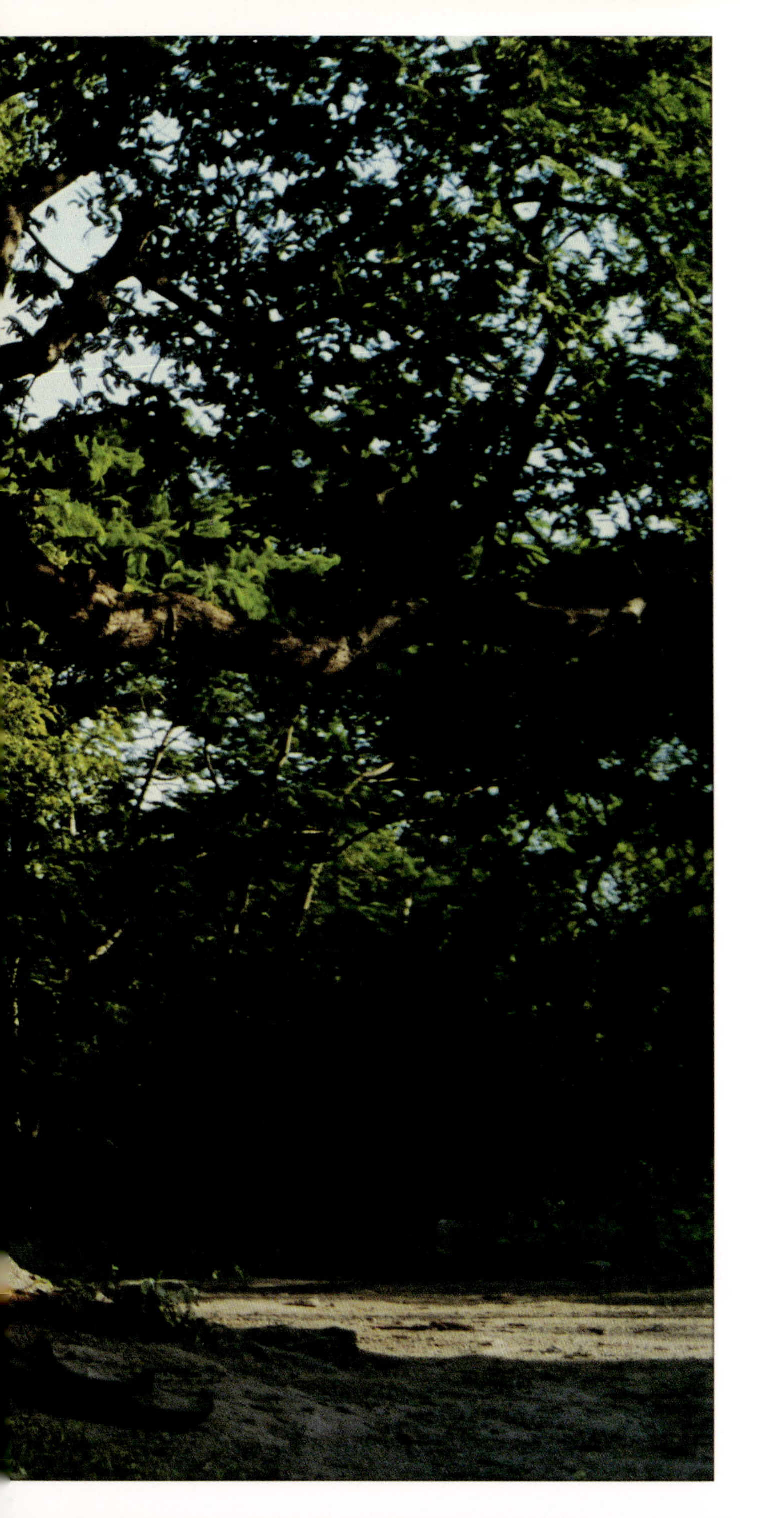

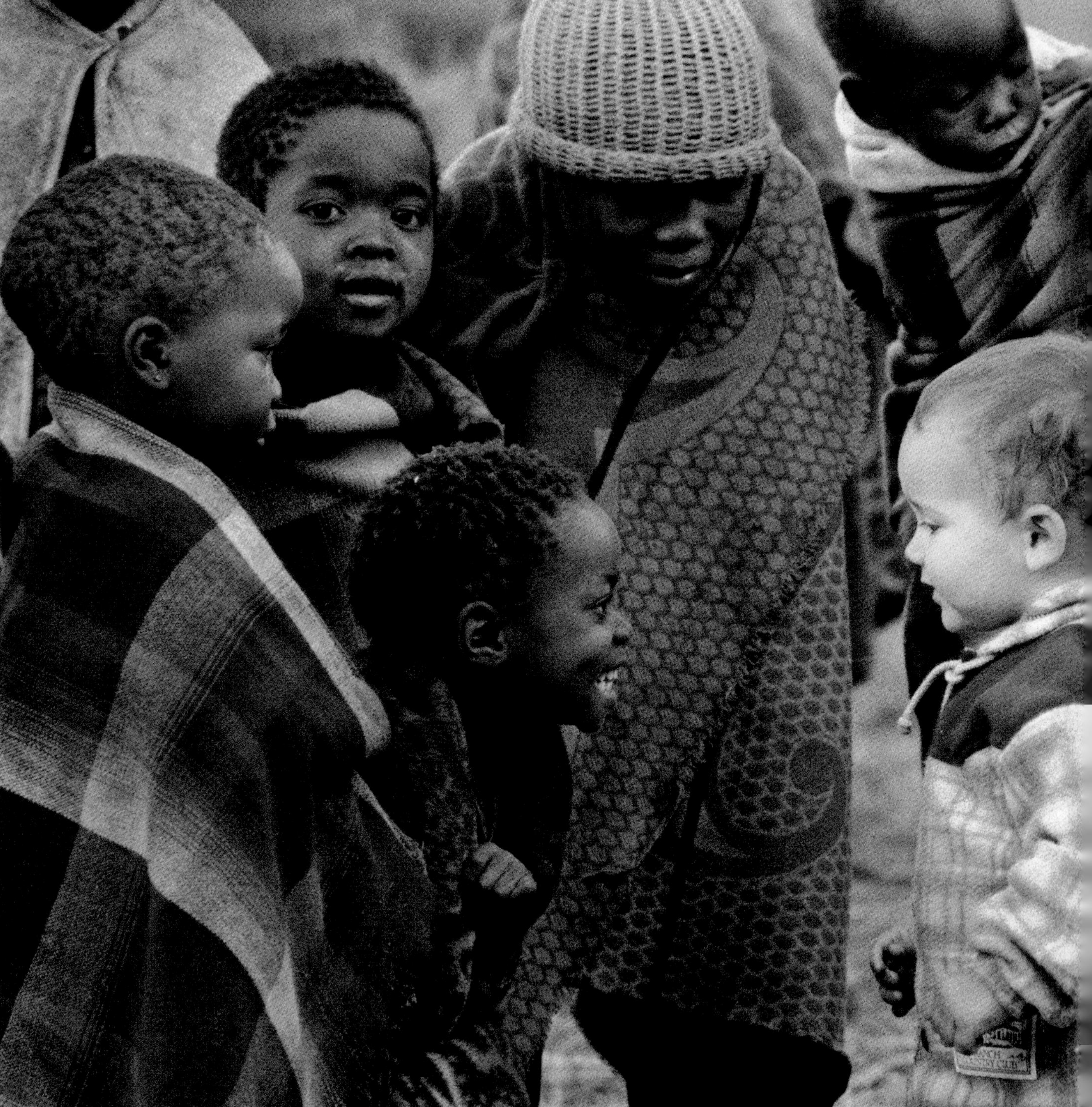

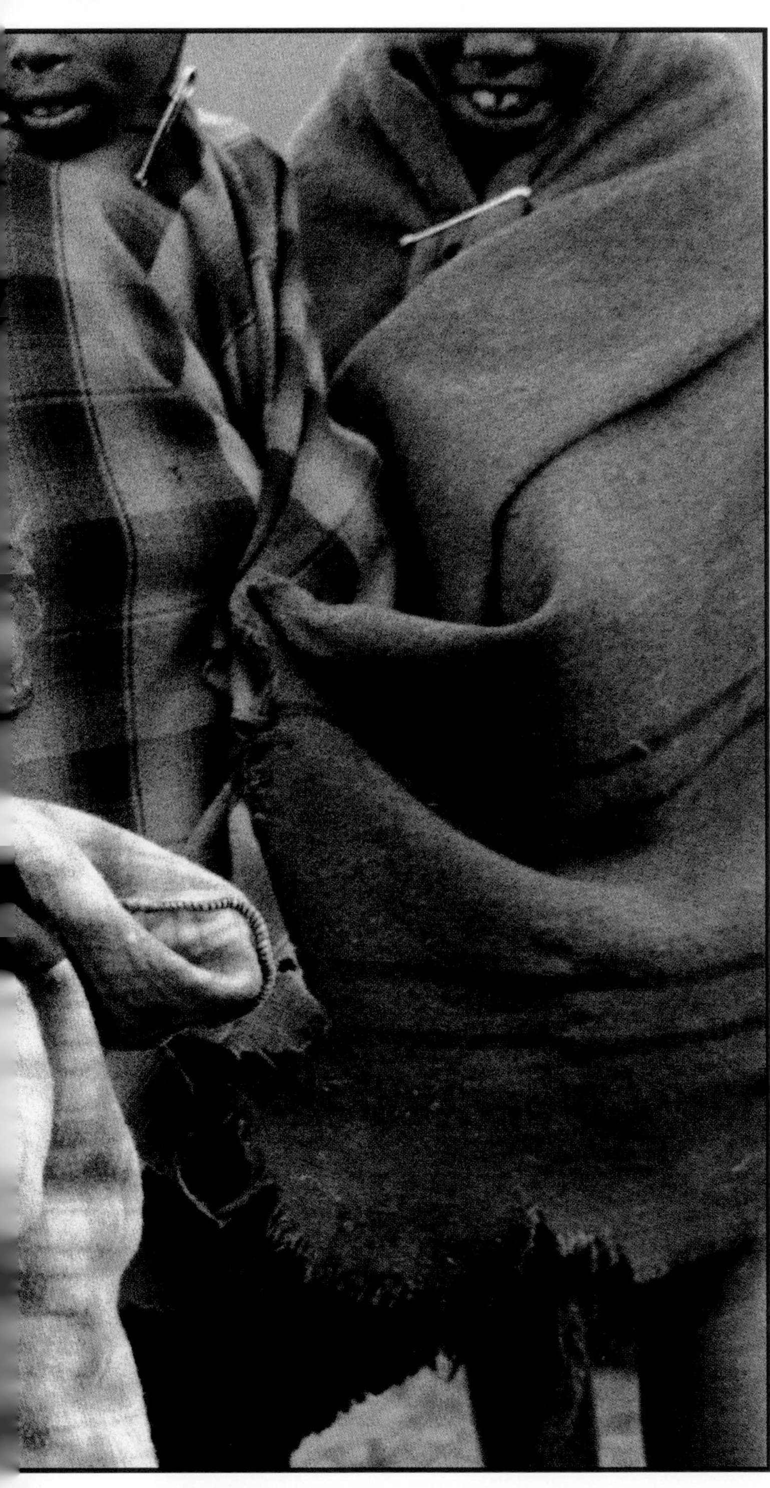

Love is but the discovery

of ourselves in others,

and the delight

in the recognition.

[ALEXANDER SMITH]

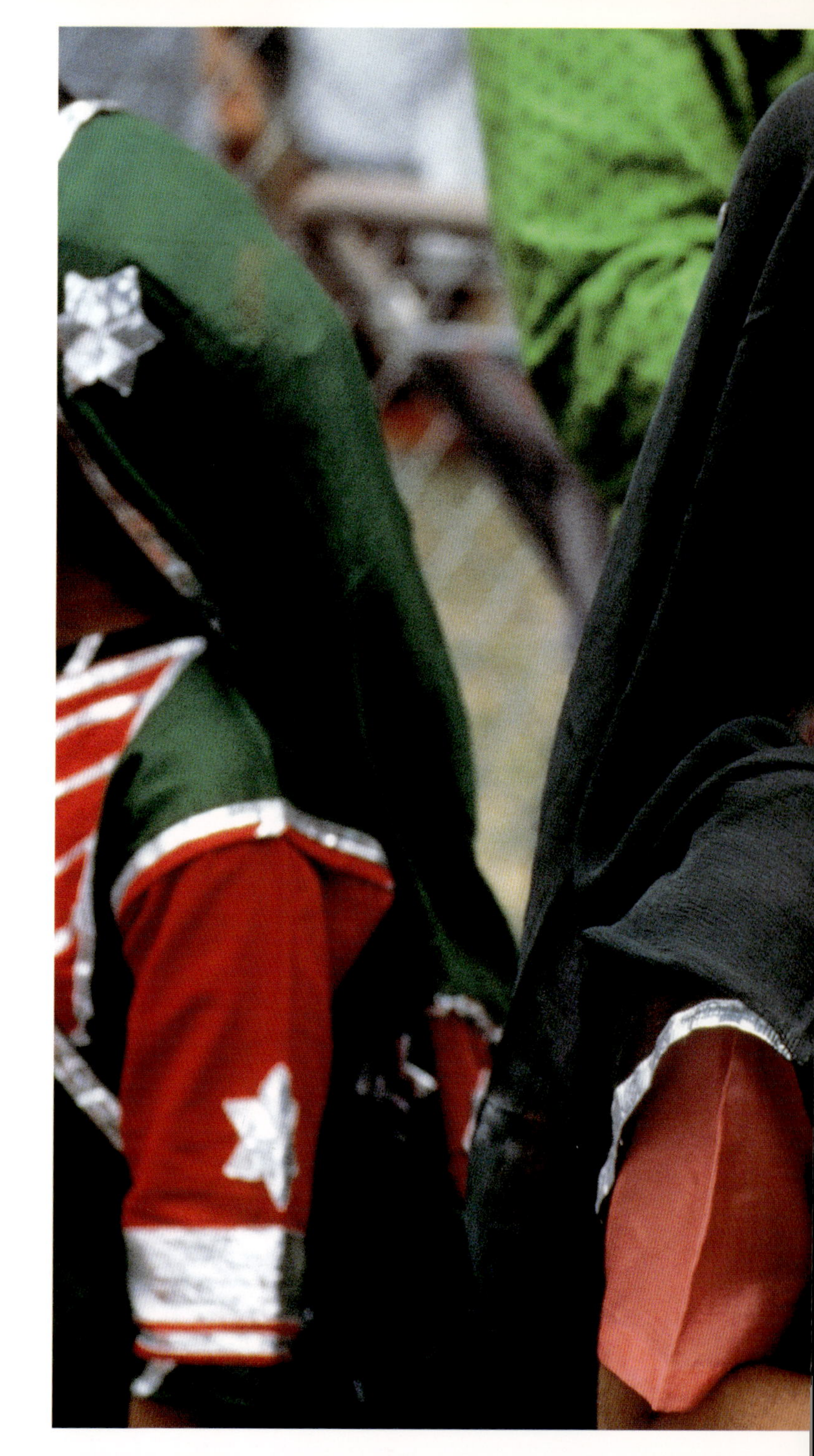

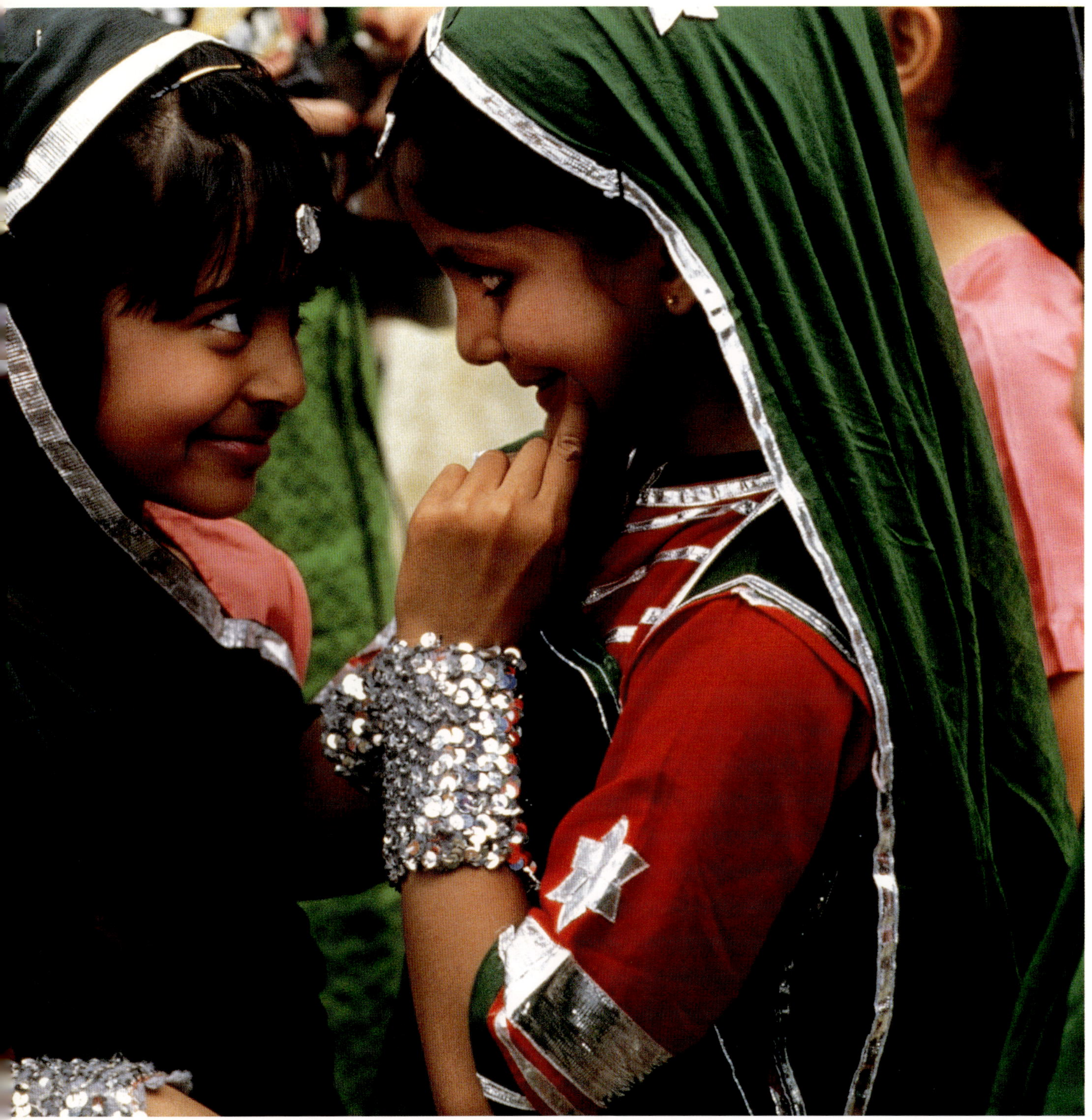

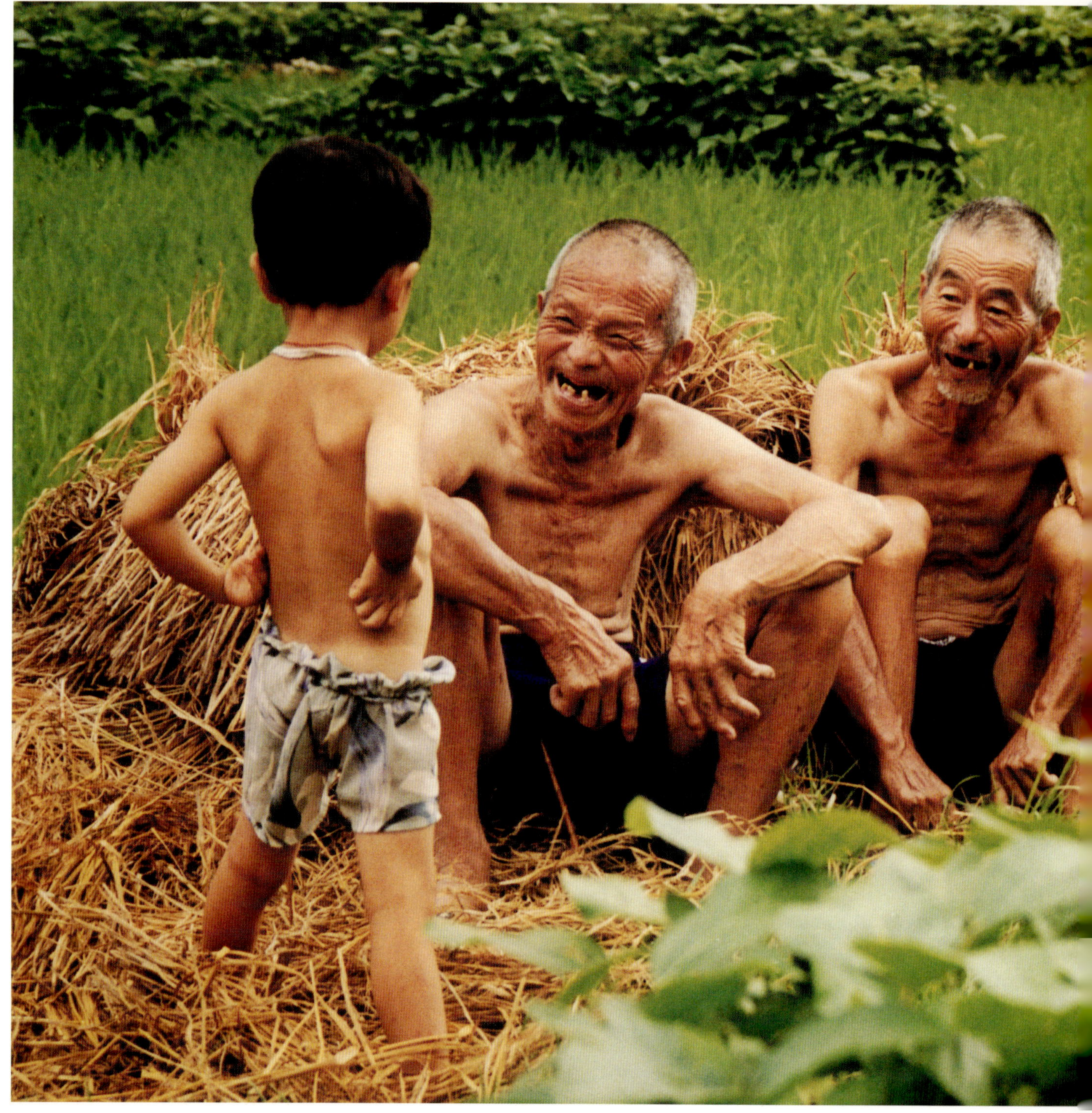

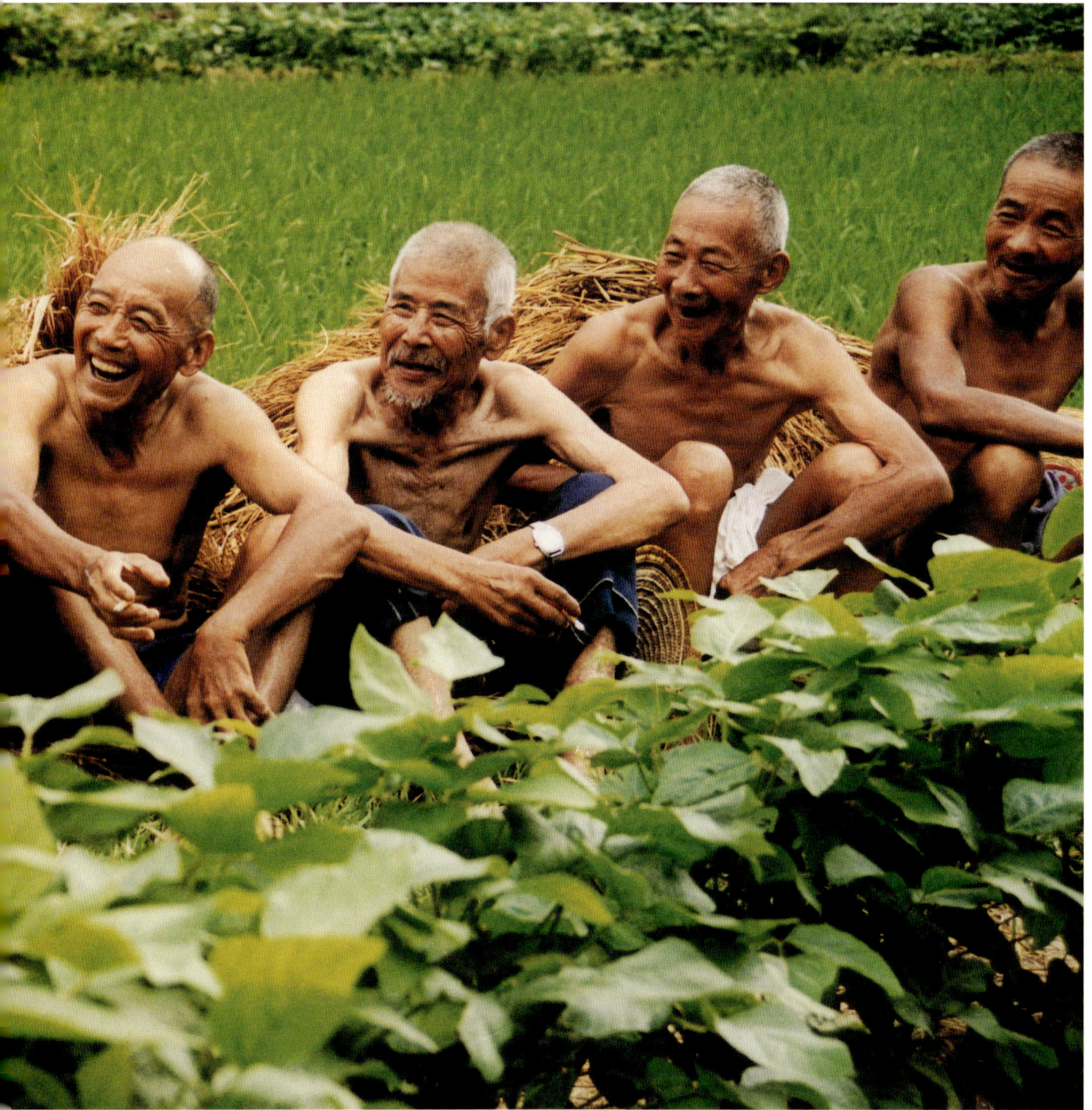

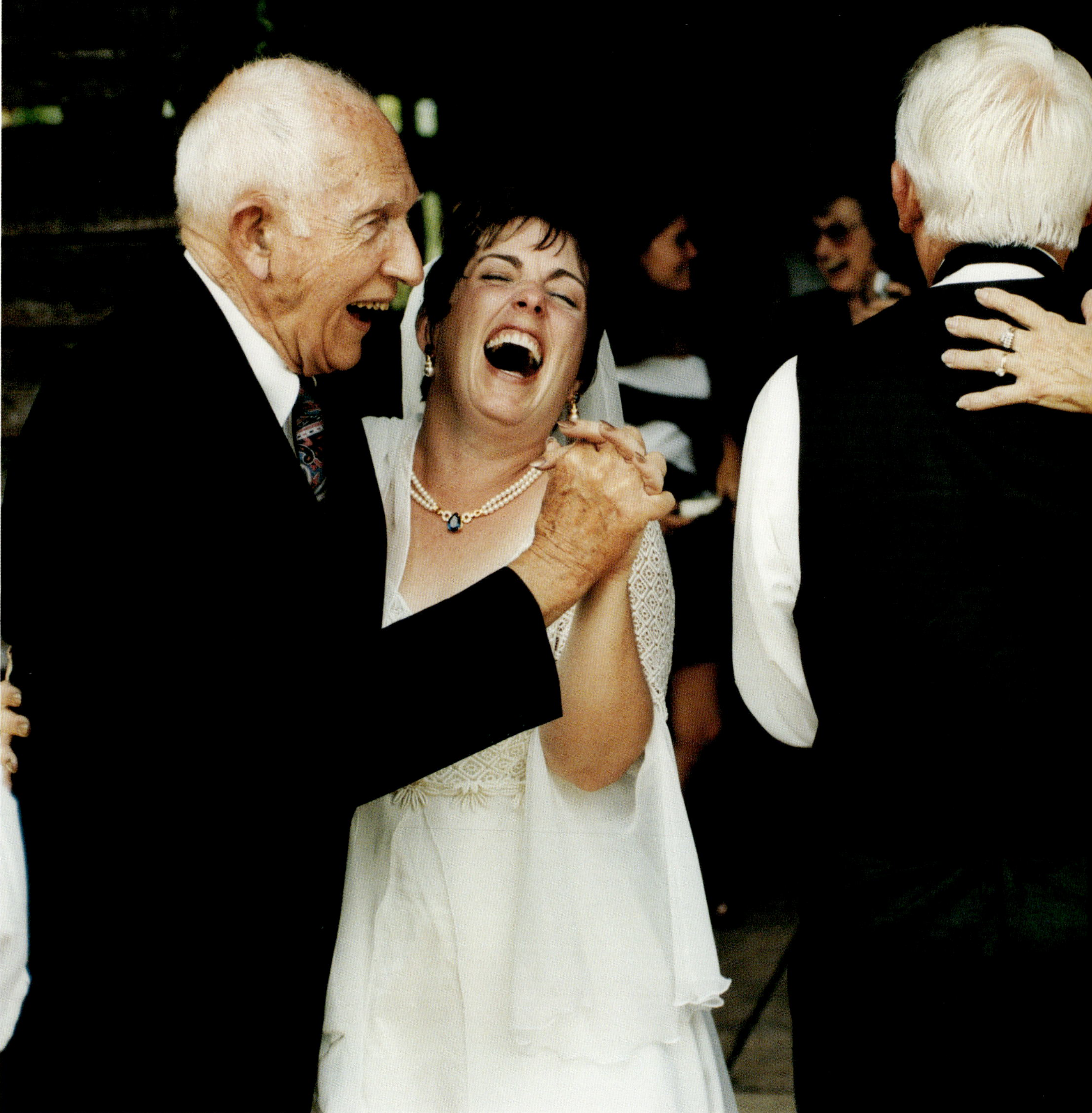

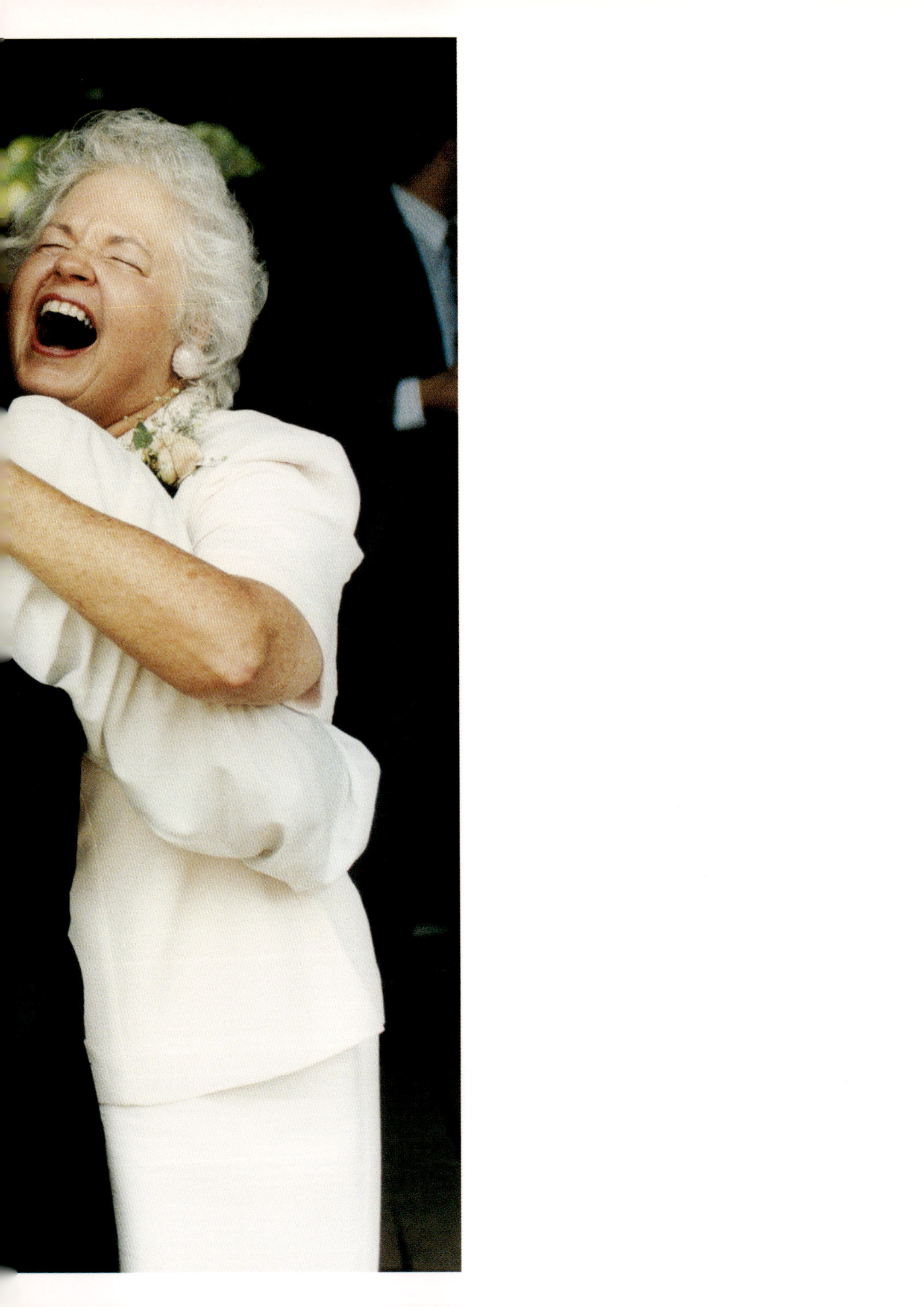

Let's do it,

let's fall in love.

[COLE PORTER]

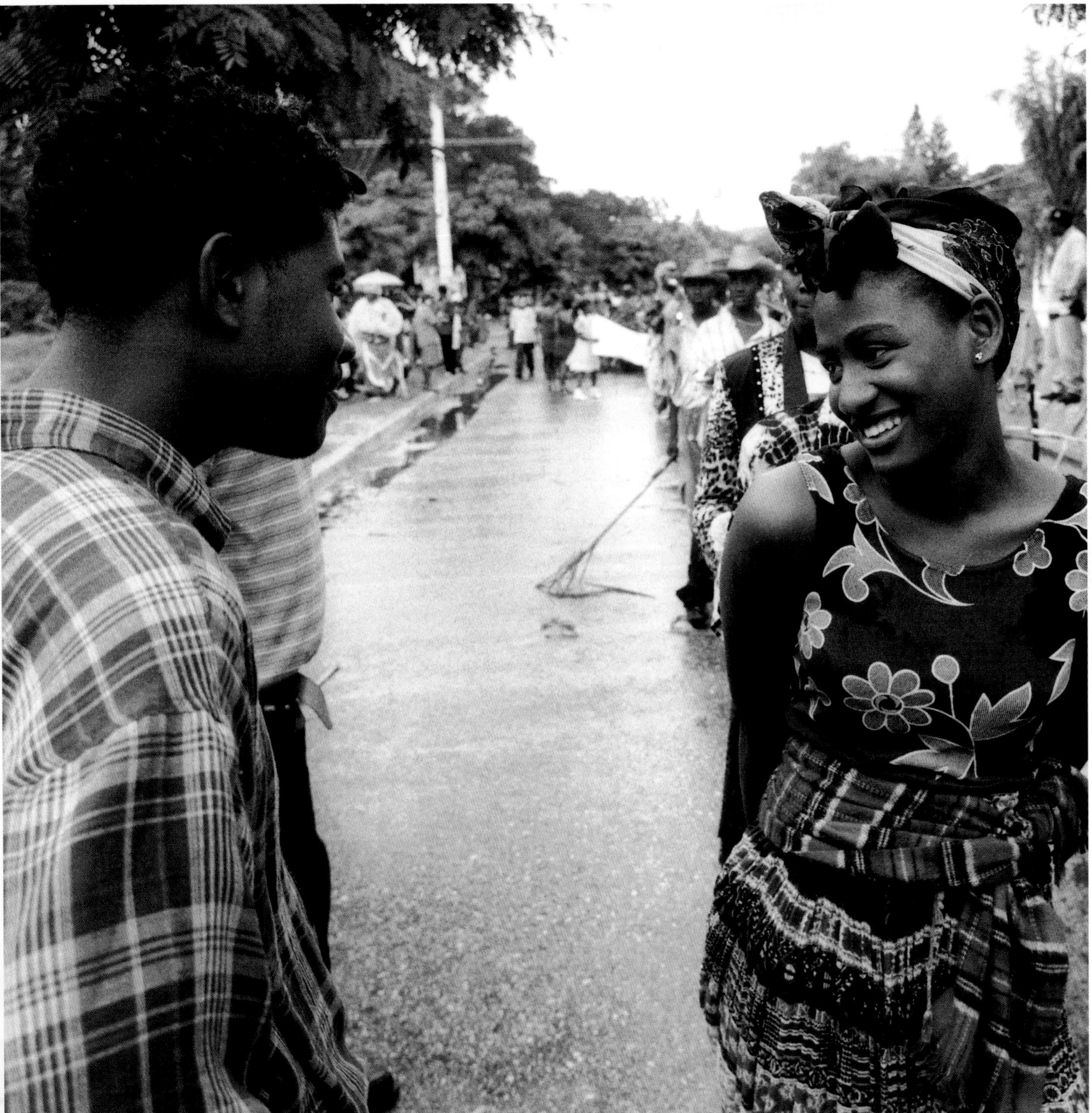

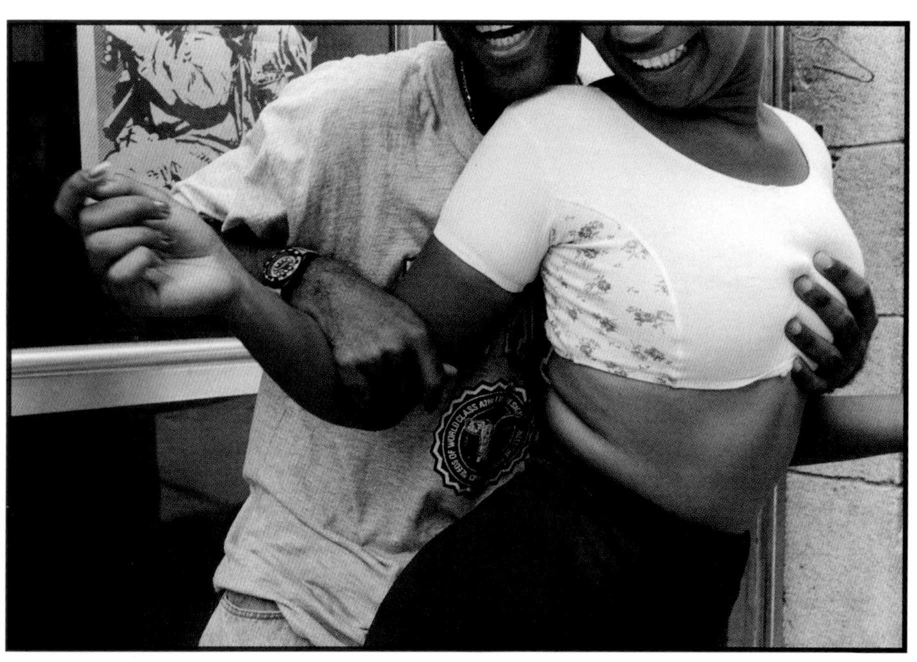

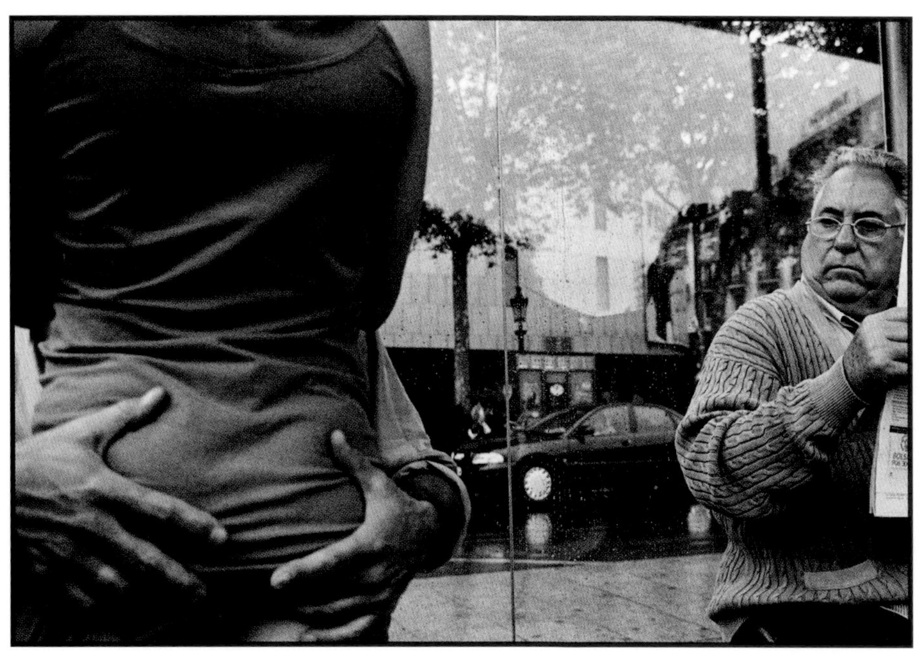

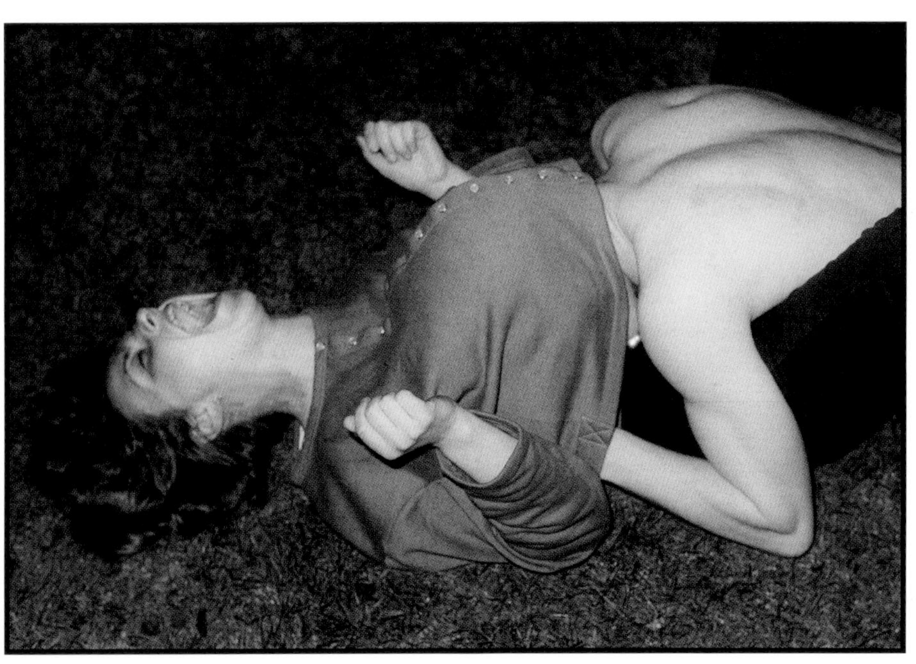

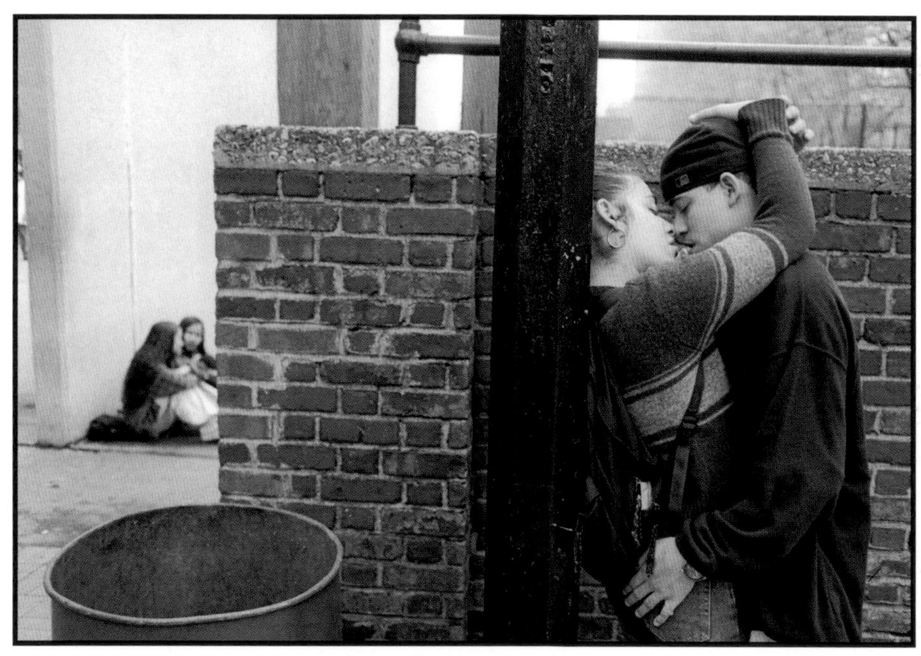

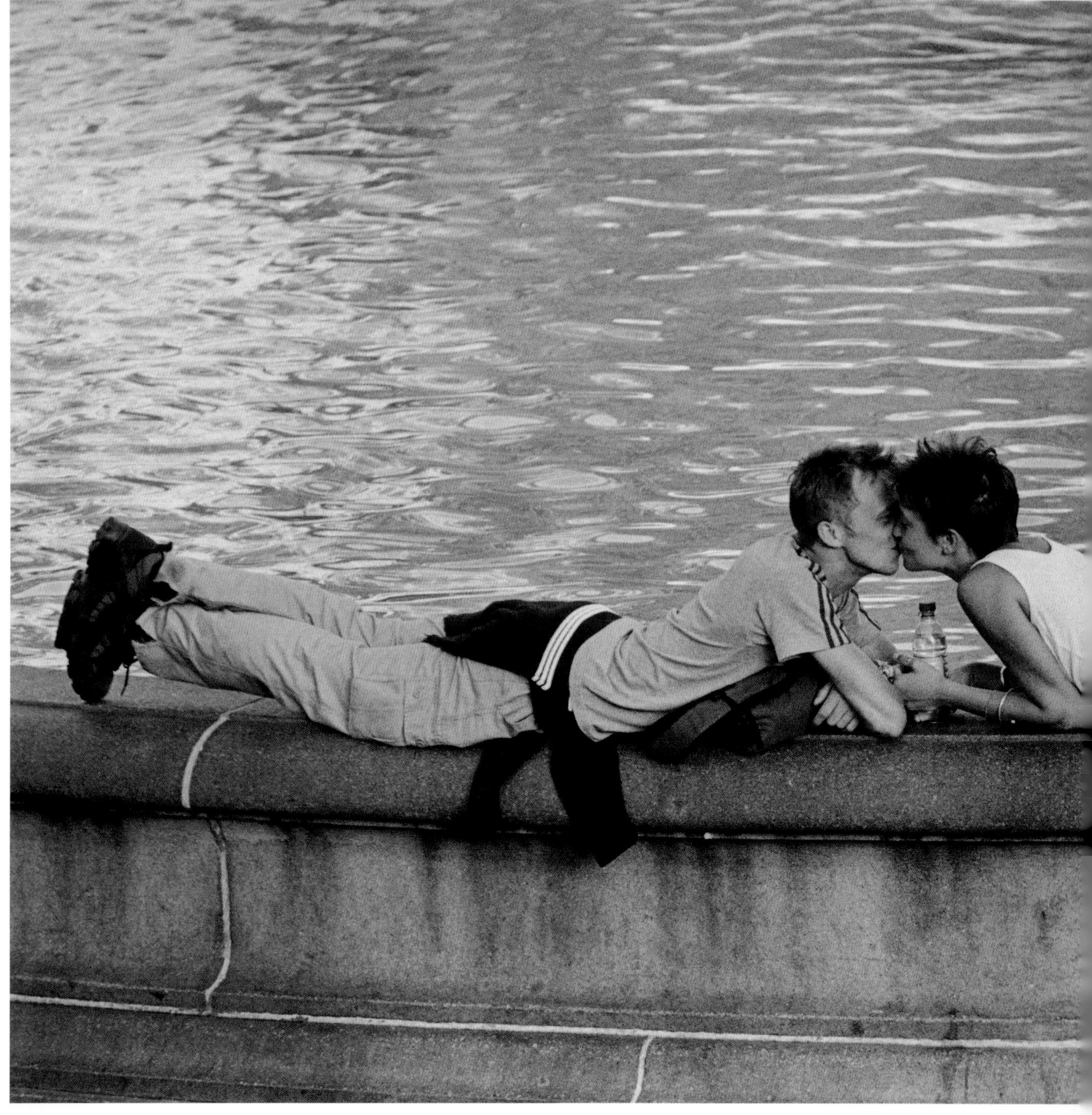

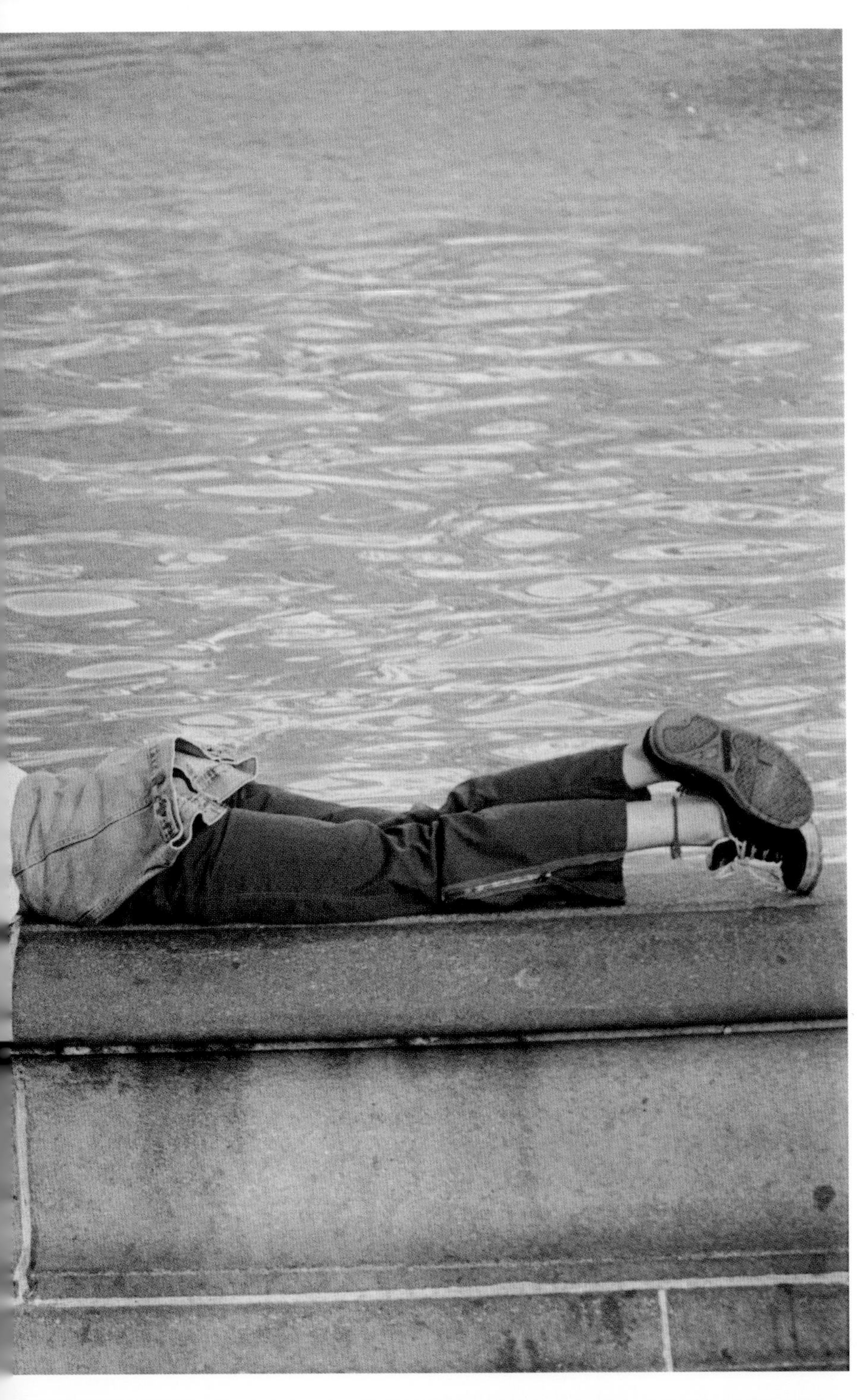

How do I love thee? Let me count the ways

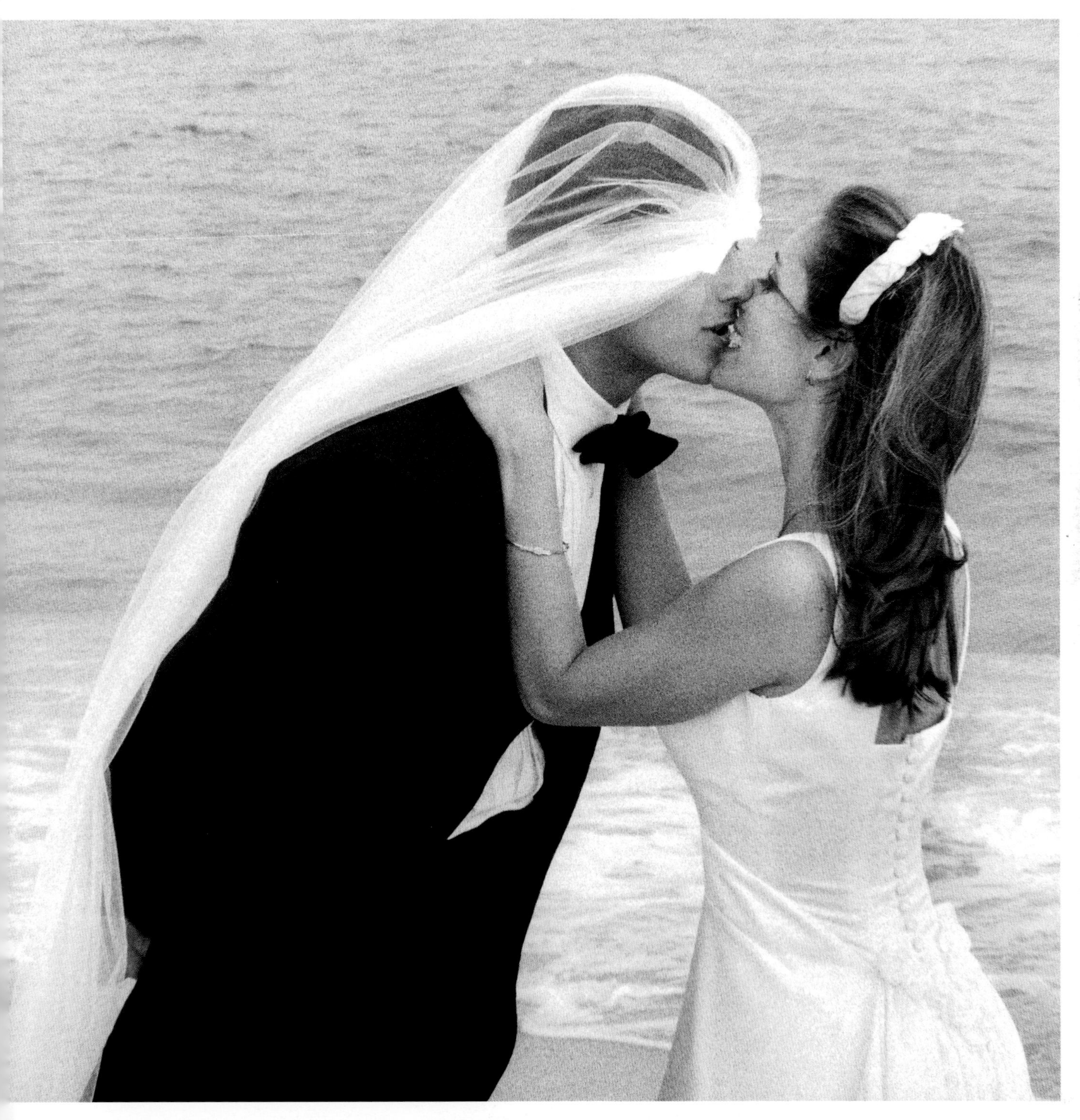

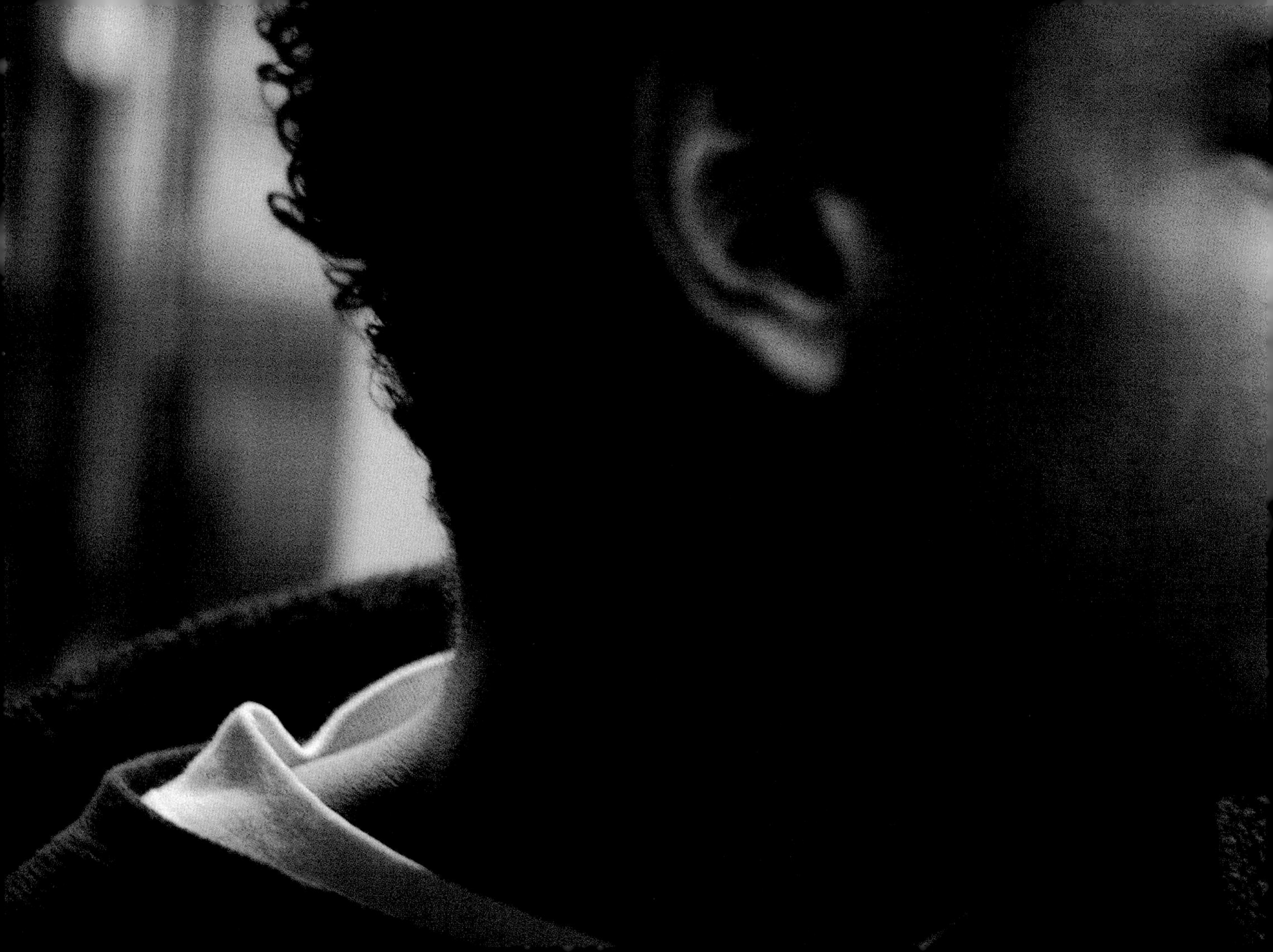

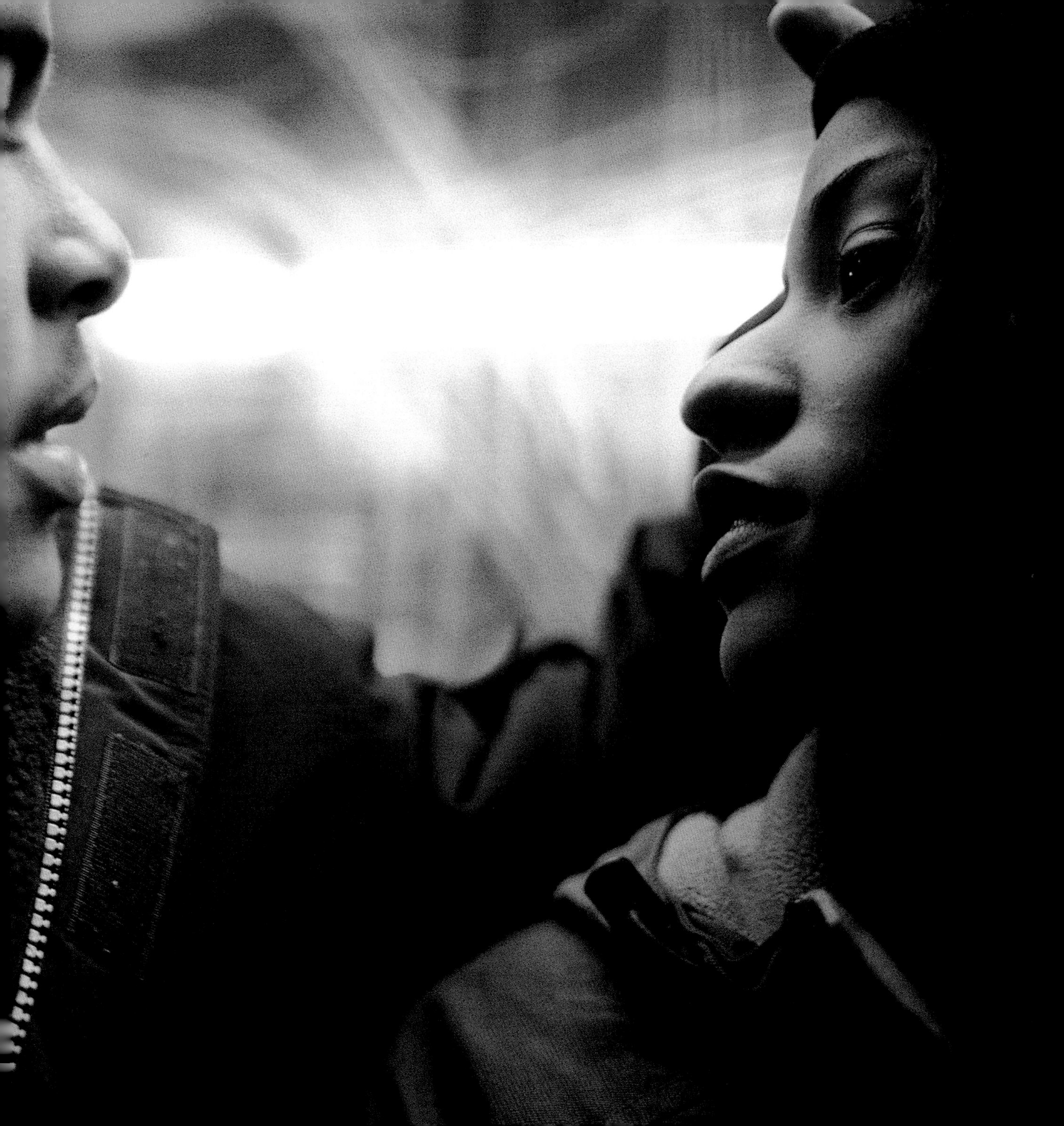

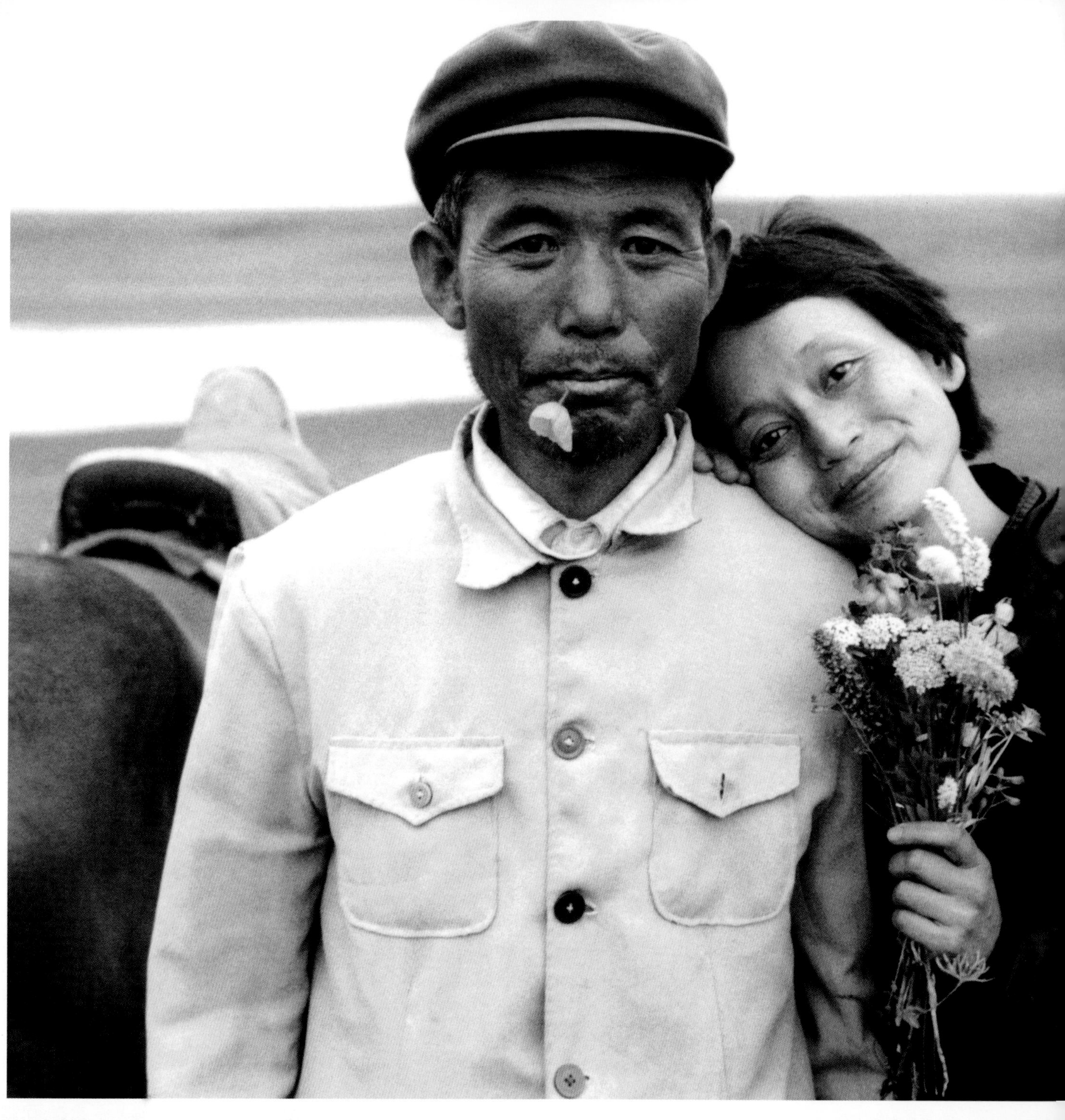

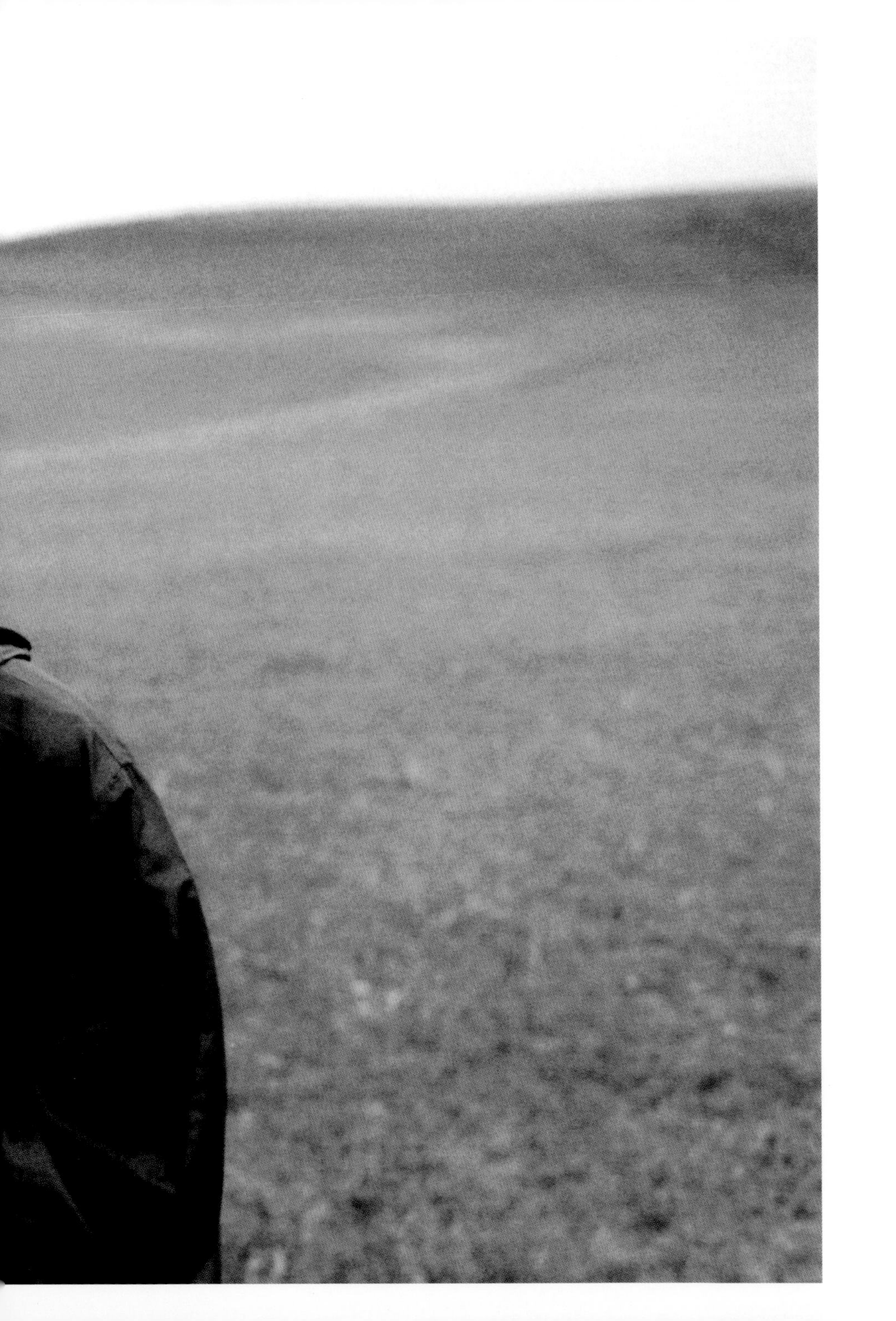

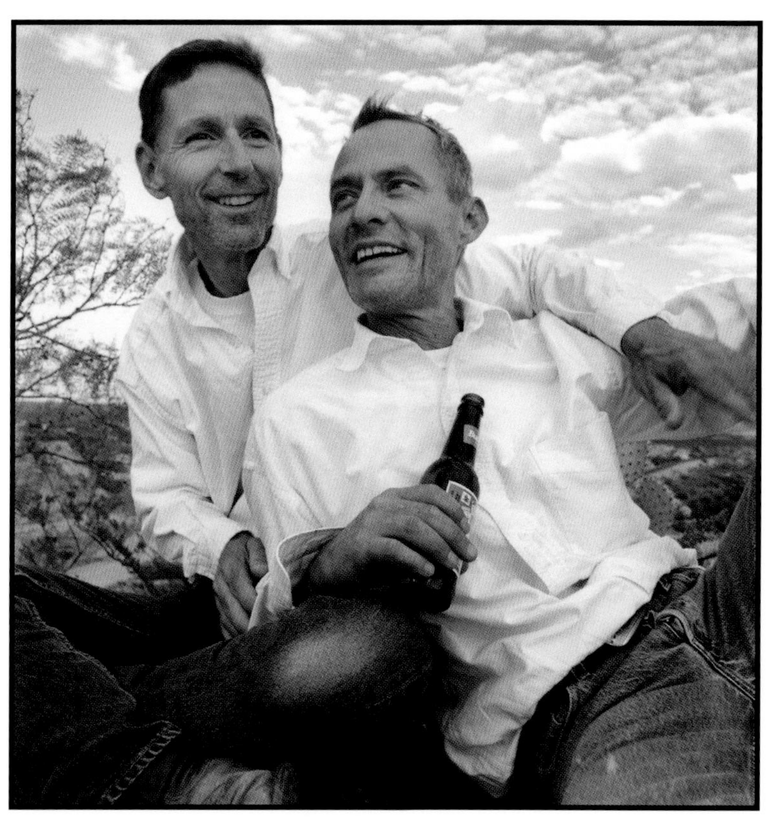

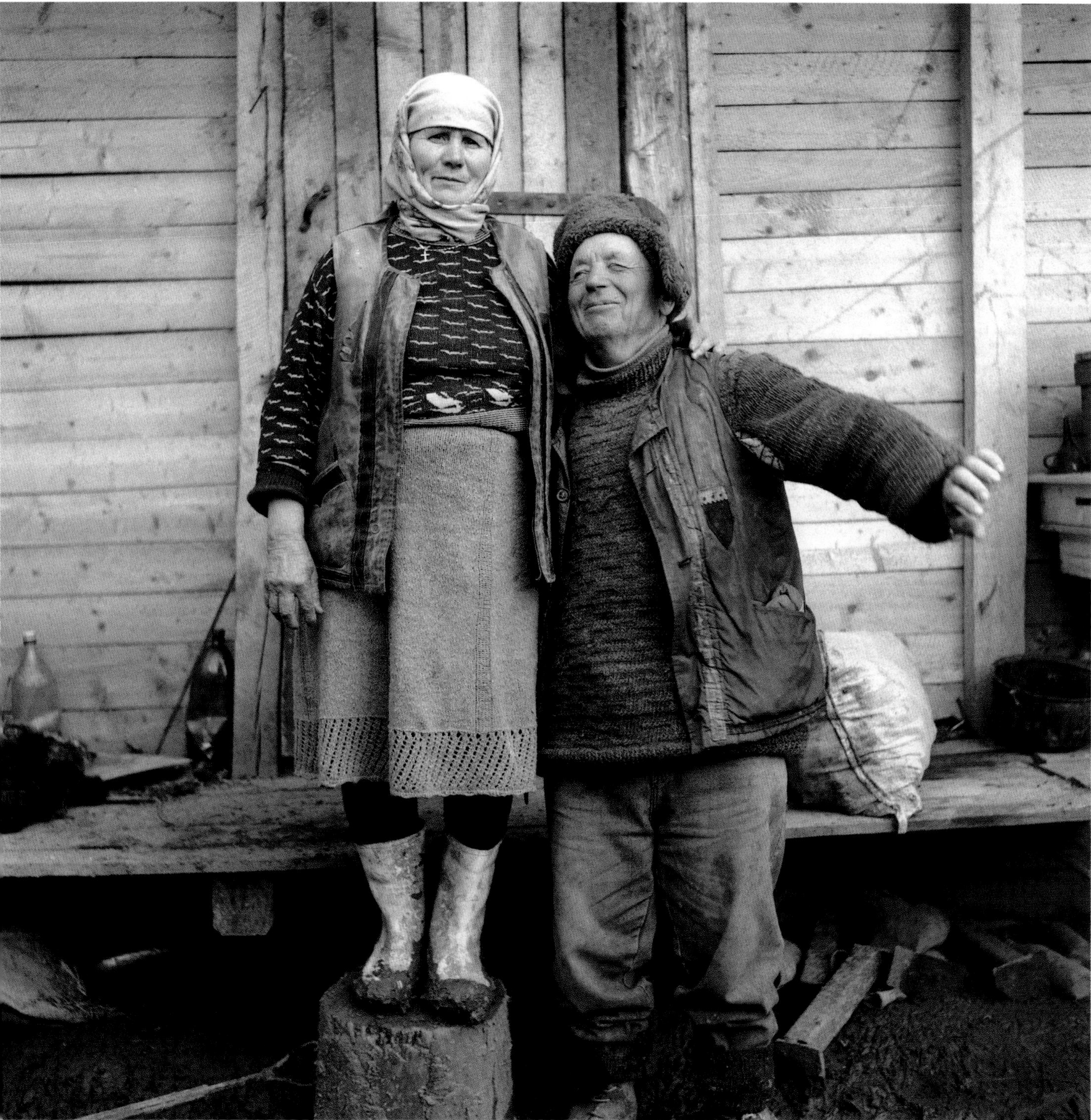

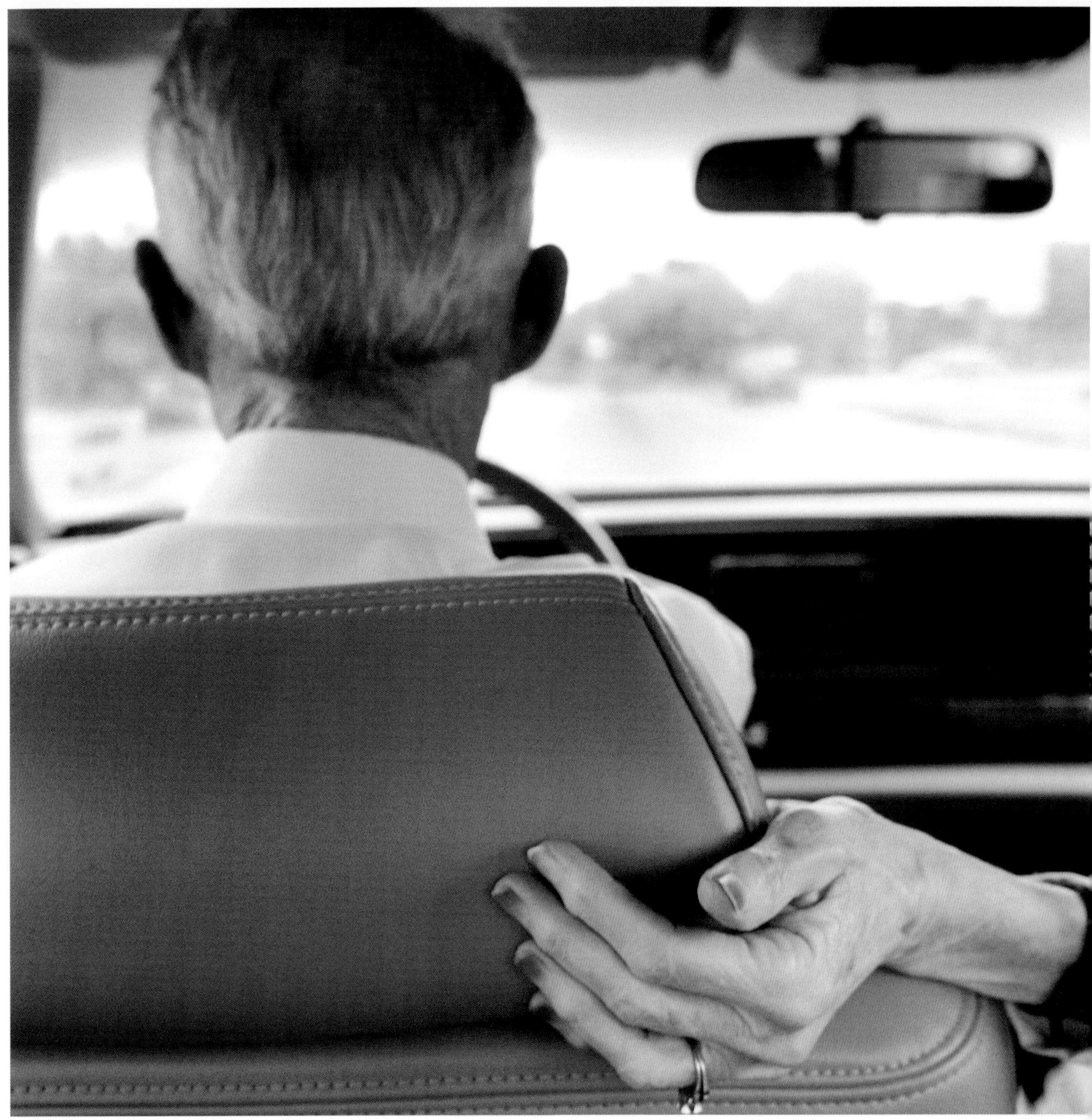

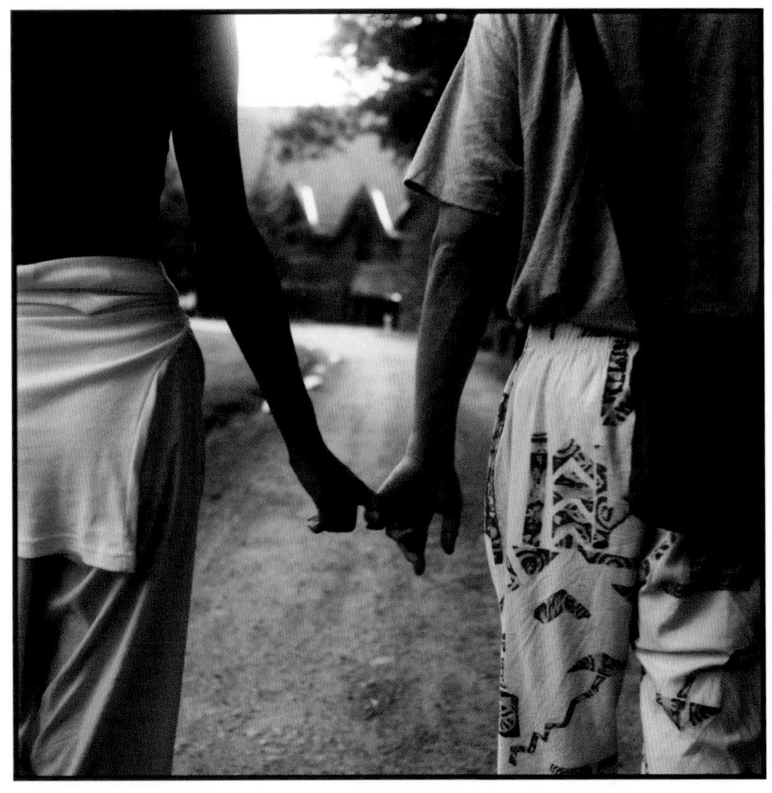

A happy marriage is a long **conversation** which always seems too short.

[ANDRE MAUROIS]

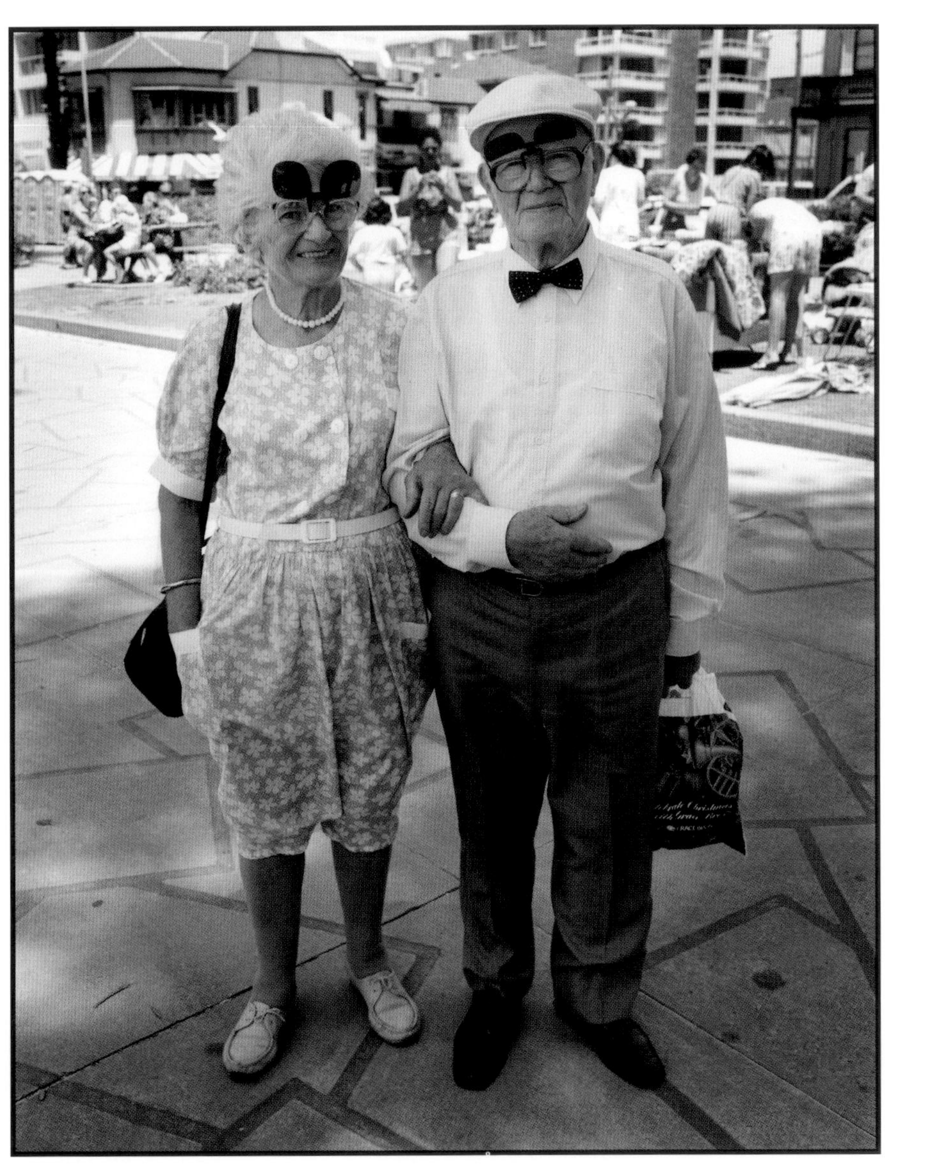

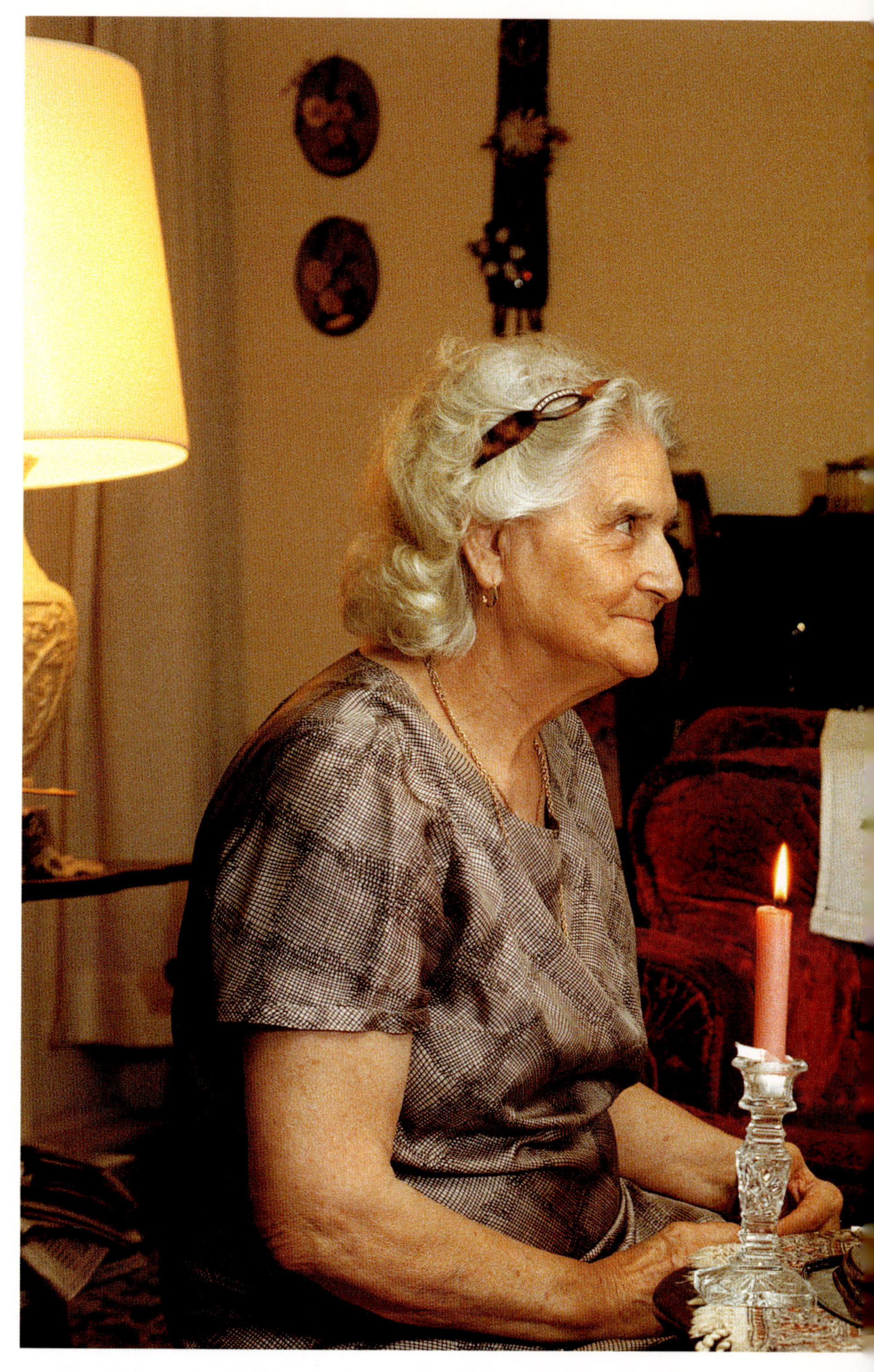

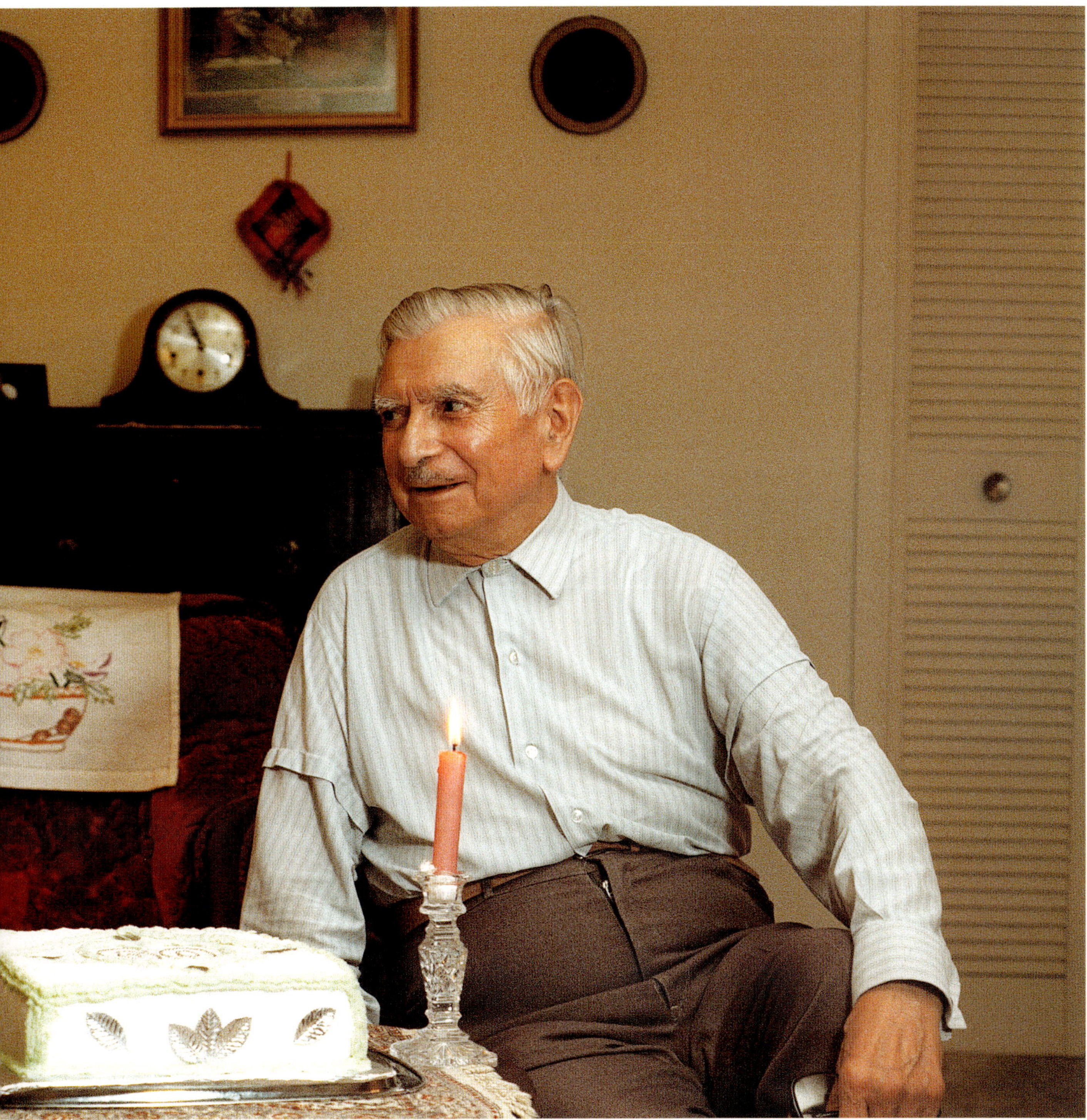

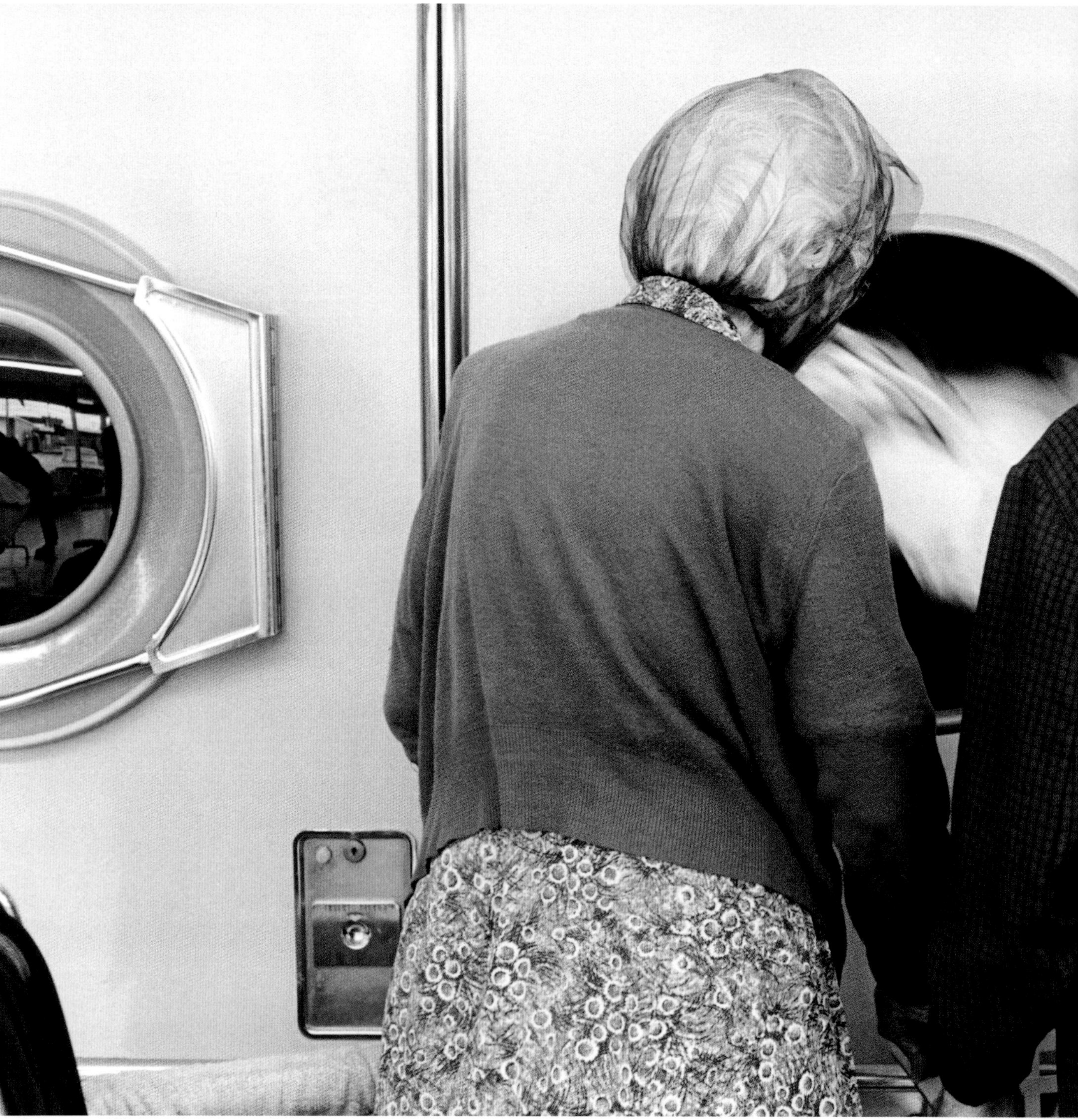

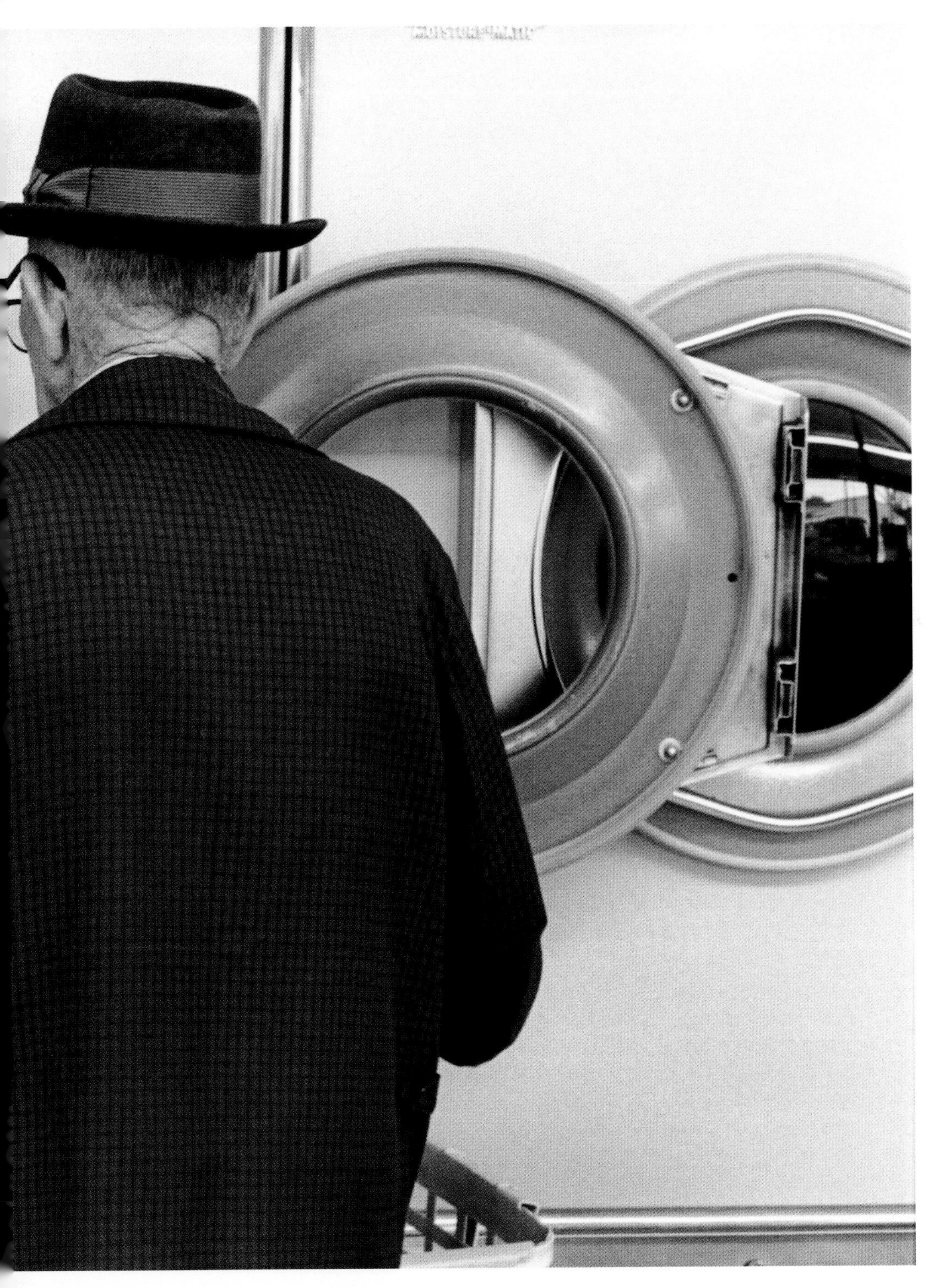

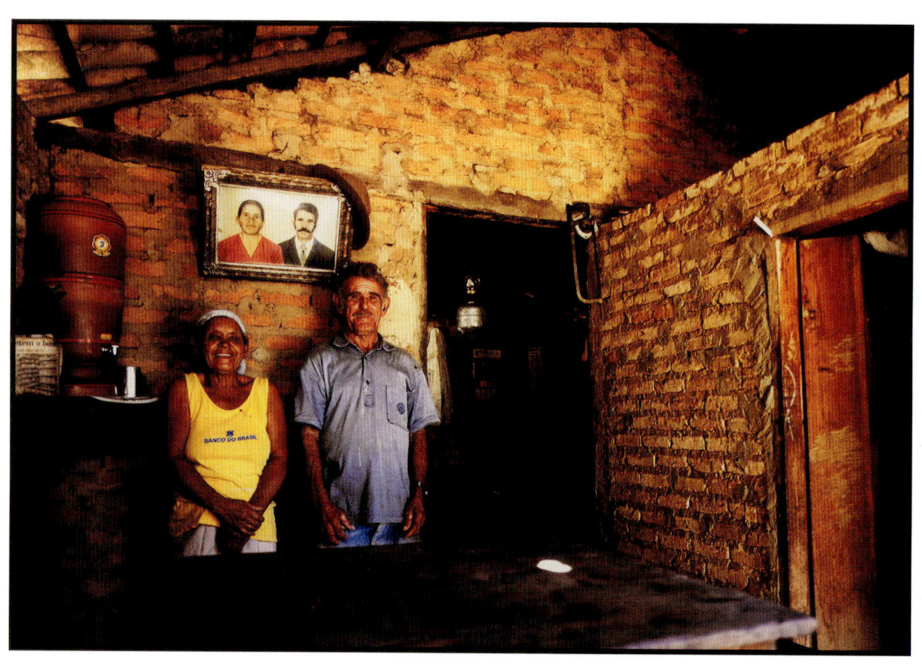
BANCO DO BRASIL

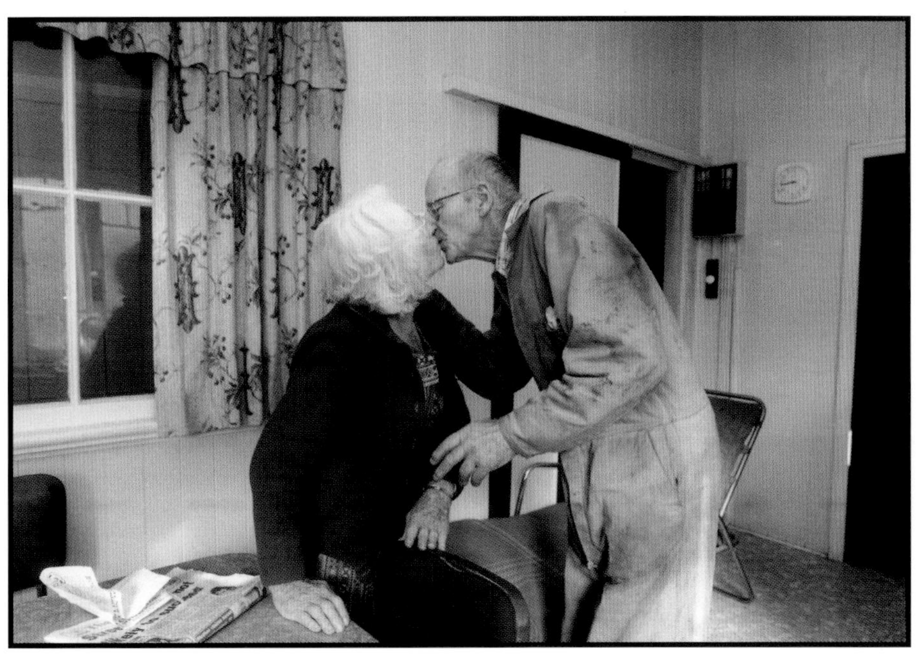

Grow old along with me, the **best** is yet to be.

[ROBERT BROWNING]

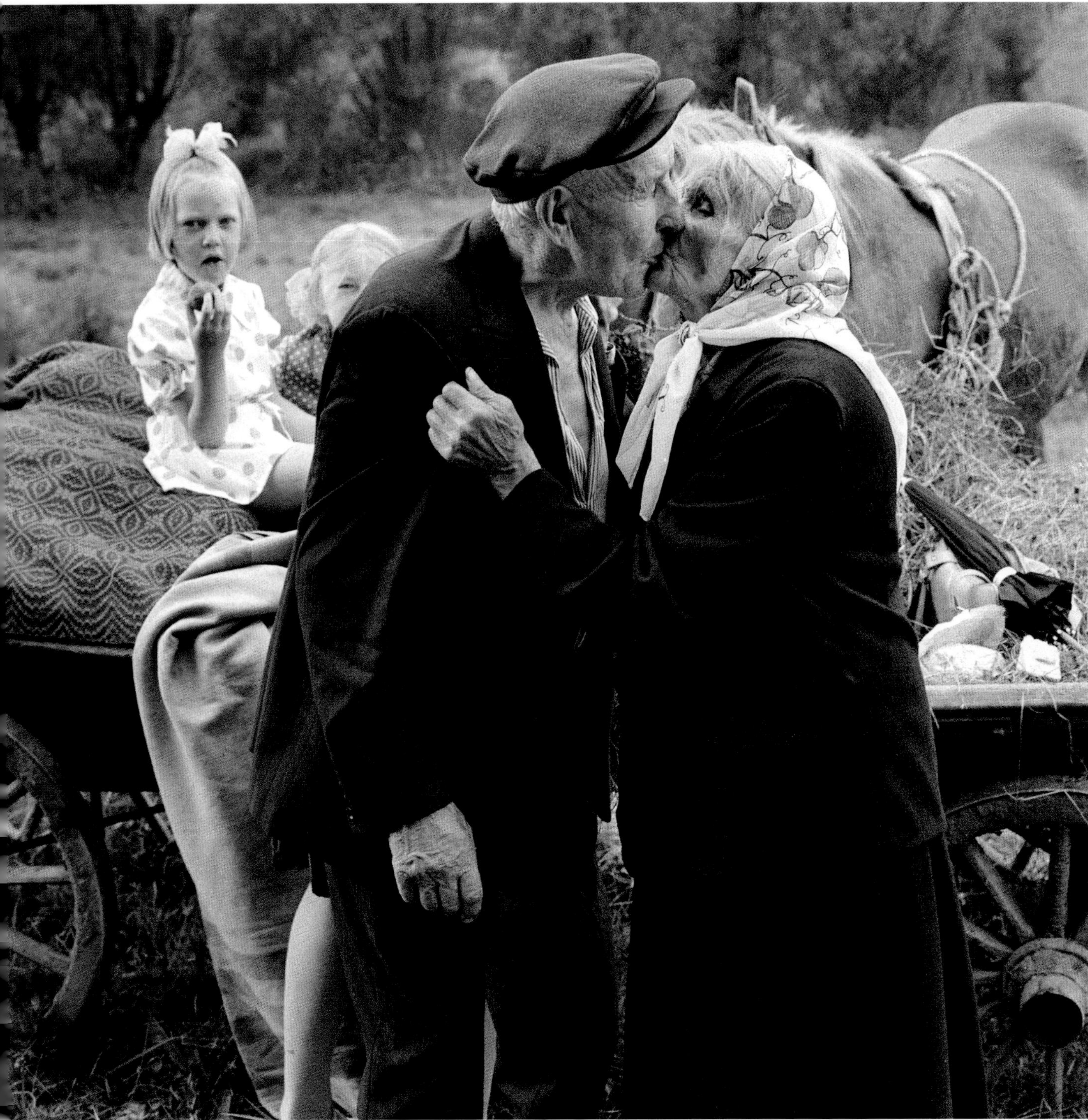

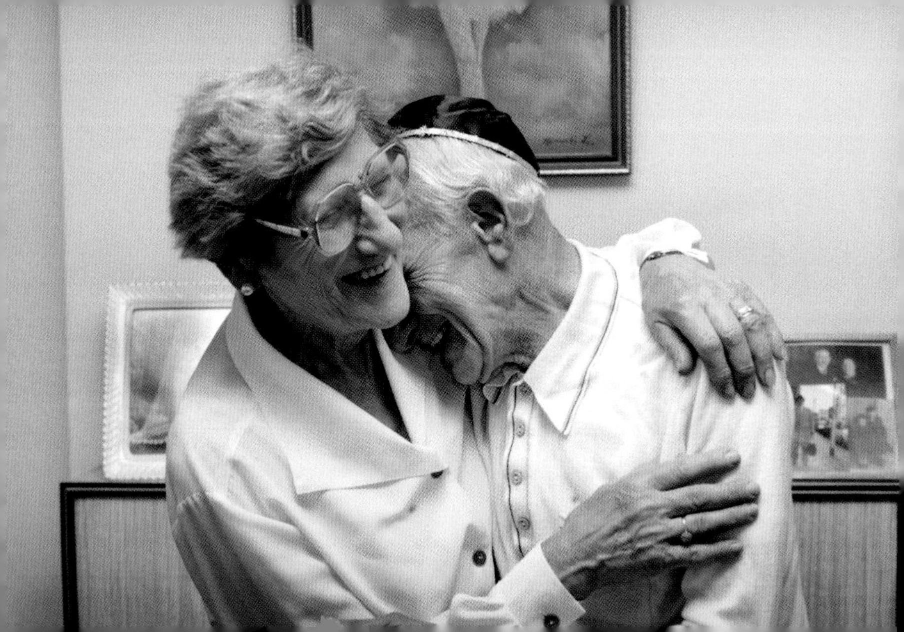

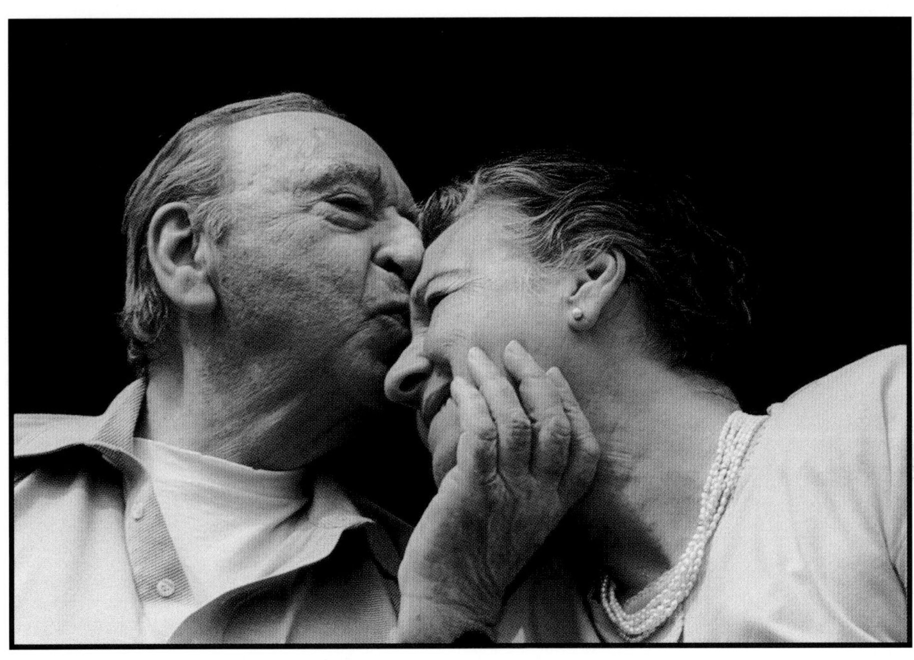

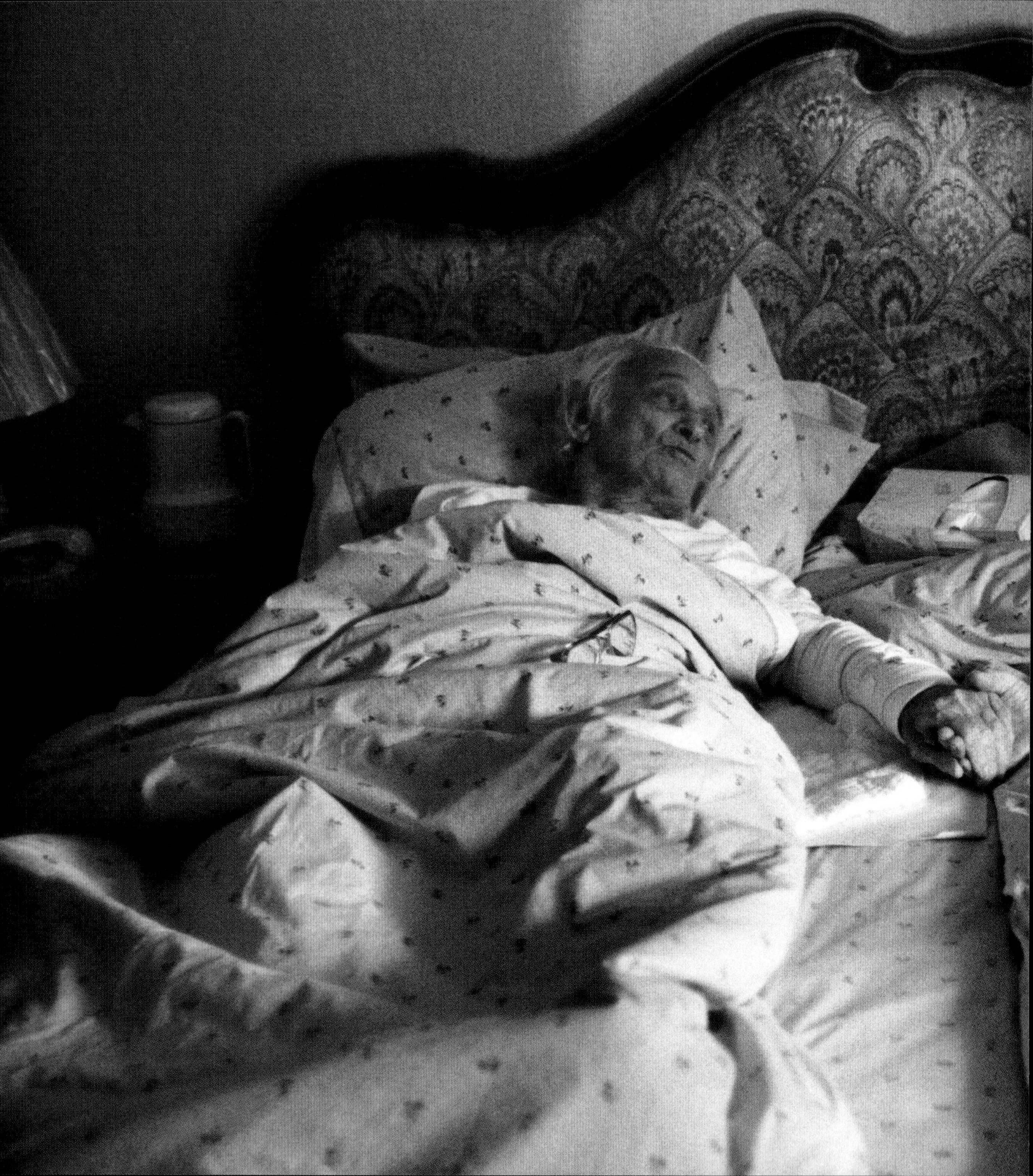

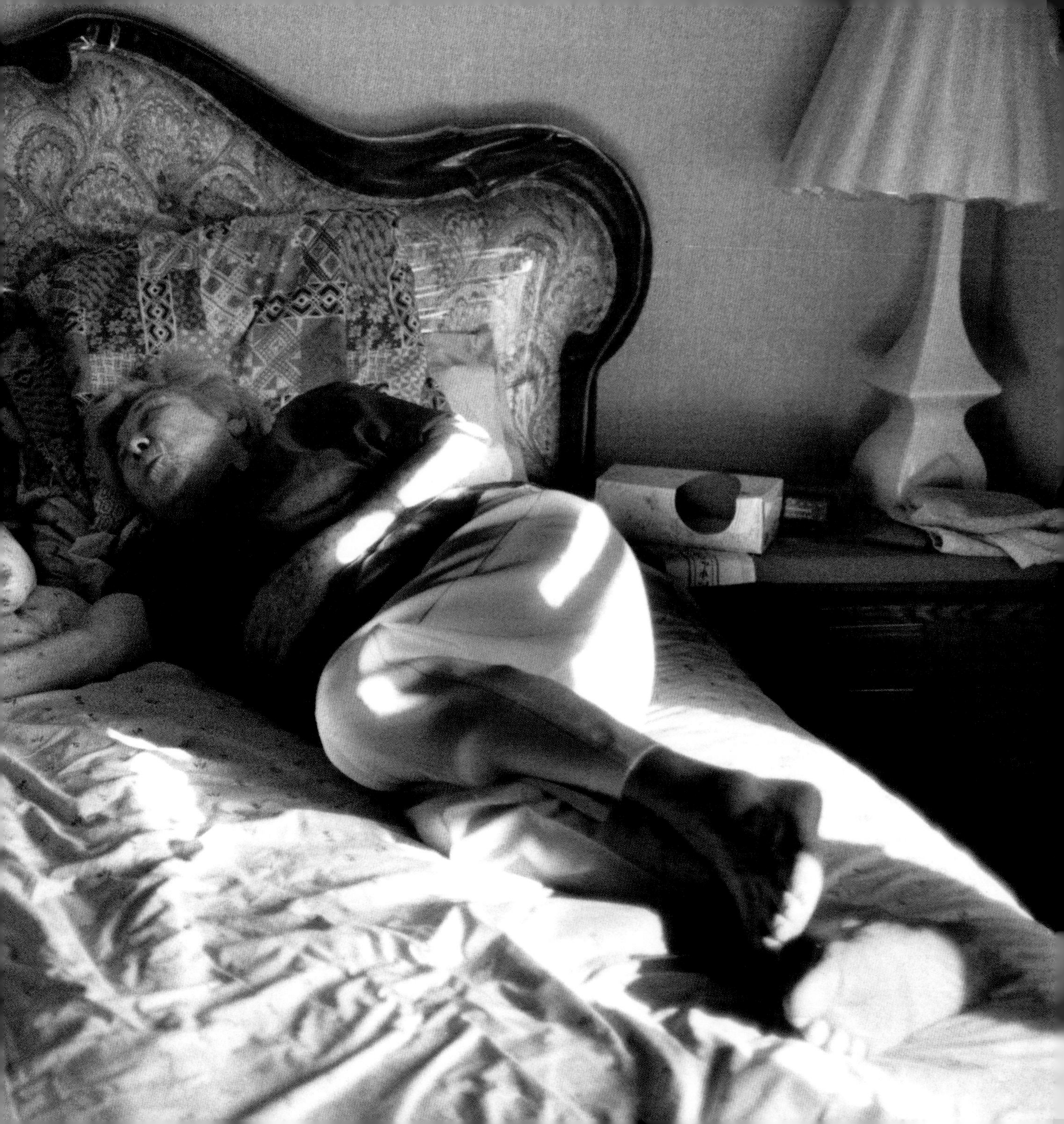

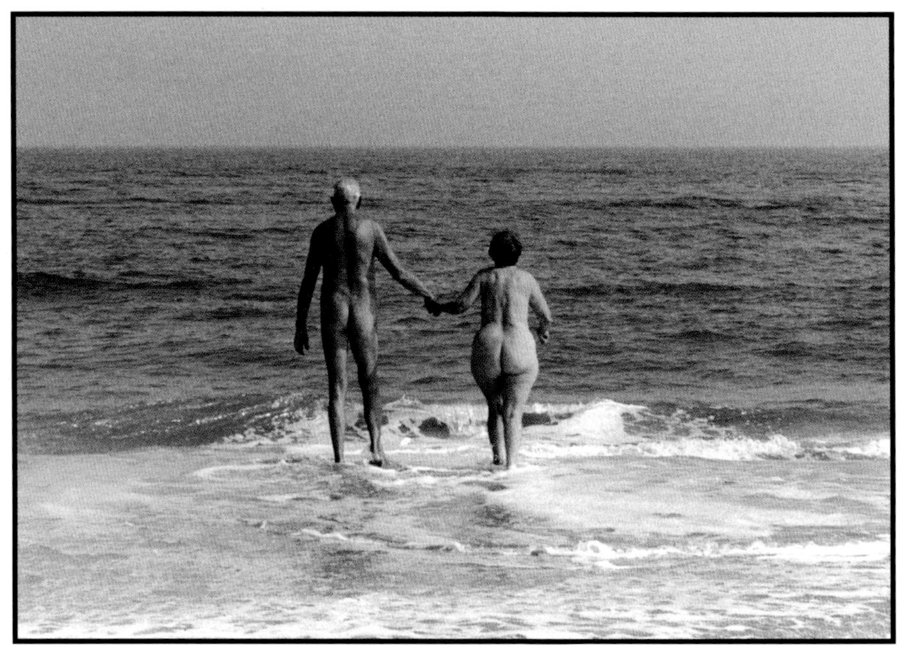

You will find as you look
back upon your life that the moments
when you have truly lived are the moments
when you have done things in the
spirit of love.

[HENRY DRUMMOND]

PHOTOGRAPHER CREDITS

IMAGE CAPTIONS

Front cover image

© Martin Langer – GERMANY
This small boy in a North Sea bay close to Husun, Germany, celebrates the joy of having the sea to himself.

Endpaper image

© Thanh Long – VIETNAM
The faces of six young friends as they take a break from lessons at their school in Phan Rang city, Vietnam.

page 2

© David M Grossman – USA
Brother and sister – six-year-old Ethan gives four-year-old Emory an enthusiastic hug at a birthday party in Brooklyn, New York.

pages 3–4

© Mikhail Evstafiev – RUSSIA
On the streets of Santiago de Cuba, Cuba – a couple's uninhibited display of affection raises a spontaneous smile from their young audience.

pages 5–6

© Amit Bar – THE NETHERLANDS
A comfortable sofa is the ideal spot for three-year-olds Allon and Tom to share laughter and play. The young friends live at the Kfar Hamaccabi Kibbutz in Israel.

page 7

© Louise Gubb – SOUTH AFRICA
The simple love of a family bonds a father and son beside the Fiherenana River in Madagascar. The Malagasy people come to this area to mine for sapphires.

pages 10–11

© Wilfred Van Zyl – SOUTH AFRICA
Six-year-old Marcelle holds on tight as her father, the photographer, takes her for a spin. To achieve the effect, Wilfred Van Zyl strapped the camera to his chest and used the self-timer to capture his daughter's delighted smile as he swings her through the air. The reflection of the photographer can be seen in the little girl's eyes.

page 15

© Gerald Botha – SOUTH AFRICA
Good morning in Durban, South Africa – the photographer's wife Aileen greets their three-month-old son Eden.

page 16

© Pepe Franco – USA
Father-to-be Angel can't help laughing as he tells a joke to his unborn baby. This image of Angel and his partner, Isabel, was captured during a family party in Aguilas, Spain.

page 17

© Slim Labidi – FRANCE
One-month-old Malik is the centre of attention for his loving parents, Cecile and Hafid, photographed at their home in Villeurbaine, France.

page 18

© Mark LaRocca – USA
A mother's joyous smile as she admires her newborn baby, Cedric, born 36 hours ago at this hospital in Newton, Massachusetts, USA.

page 19

© Milo Stewart Jr – USA
In Cooperstown, New York, new mother Leslie is enchanted with her baby son Bartow.

page 21

© Michael Decher – GERMANY
"Klara and me" – this self-portrait captures a father's face full of tenderness and love as he holds his one-week-old daughter.

pages 22–23

© Shannon Eckstein – CANADA
Rubbing noses in Vancouver, Canada – new father Davy finds the perfect way to bond with his baby daughter, Ciara, only nine days old.

page 24

© Abel Naim – VENEZUELA
During a workshop for the underprivileged communities of Caracas, Venezuela, children learn how to communicate with others and to express their emotions. As the instructor, Durbin, gives her young student a hug, their faces light up with love and happiness.

page 25

© Jane Wyles – NEW ZEALAND
Laughter is infectious for father and son, Drew and James, as they share an affectionate hug in Christchurch, New Zealand.

page 26

© John McNamara – USA
The Special Olympics in Union City, California – father Daryl gives his son, JR, a hug full of love and pride after the young competitor finishes his event.

page 27

© Marc Rochette – CANADA
A look of love and encouragement from father to daughter. Six-year-old Erica's soccer team from Bramalea, Canada, may not win very often, but her father is always on hand to support her efforts in the game.

page 28

© Christel Dhuit – NEW ZEALAND
They may be twins, but their reactions are very different. Five-month-old sisters in Auckland, New Zealand.

page 29

© Philip Kuruvita – AUSTRALIA
A woodshed in Tasmania, Australia, provides an unusual playground for identical twins, Summer and Melody.

pages 30–31

© Steven Siewert – AUSTRALIA
An Aboriginal brother and sister can't hold back the smiles as their photograph is taken in Queensland, Australia.

pages 32–33

© Martin Rosenthal – ARGENTINA
A father and his children in Juanchaco, Colombia.

page 34

© Victor Englebert – USA
In the Amazon rainforest of Brazil, a Yanomami Indian relaxes in a hammock made of bark strips and plays with his young grandson.

page 35

© Jim Witmer – USA
A photographer father takes a self-portrait with his one-year-old son, Adam, at home in Troy, Ohio, USA.

pages 36–37

© Marcy Appelbaum – USA
In Jacksonville, Florida, USA, two-year-old Rachel is curious to see if her belly button matches her father's.

page 38

© Gordon Trice – USA
Father Heath holds his eight-month-old daughter, Bethany. This family portrait was photographed in Abilene, Texas, USA.

page 39

© Ray Peek – AUSTRALIA
Another generation learns about mustering from the head of the family. "Big" Morrie Dingle, a grazier in South Queensland, Australia, and his two grandsons take a break from the saddle to enjoy some food.

page 40

© Lyn Dowling – AUSTRALIA
"Ma" and me – Rebecca, aged 20 months, and her grandmother "Ma" share the simple pleasures of a street festival in Brisbane, Australia.

page 41

© David Williams – UK
Face to face – in Newcastle, England, godfather David meets his one-month-old godson, Samuel, for the first time.

page 43

© Georgina Lucock – AUSTRALIA
A quiet moment – parents Kevin and Annette tenderly embrace 10-month-old Jai during a family photo session in Bellingen, Australia.

pages 44–45

© Edmond Terakopian – UK
A family is reunited. British Royal Air Force sergeant John has just returned from the Gulf War to his wife Sharon and their two-year-old son Phillip. Their reunion was captured during a press conference in Stanmore, Middlesex, England.

page 46

© Eddee Daniel – USA
A moment of discovery in Sauk City, Wisconsin, USA, as one-year-old Chelsea realises where the music is coming from.

page 47

© Shauna Angel Blue – USA
Chicago, Illinois, USA – dressed in her favourite tutu, two-year-old Rose dances to the tune of her mother's harp.

pages 48–49

© Russell Shakespeare – AUSTRALIA
In Manly, New South Wales, Australia, five-month-old Camille has a captive audience in her mother, Toni, and visiting grandparents, Margaret and Handley.

page 50

© Thomas Patrick Kiernan – IRELAND
A young boy shares his delight with his mother, as he paddles in the water on Coney Island, New York.

page 51

© Neil Selkirk – USA
Open wide – on a trip to the beach in Wellfleet, Massachusetts, USA, nothing interests Zane more than her mother, Susan.

pages 52–53

© Lydia Linda Ruscitto – ITALY
Nose to nose – as brother and sister Alessandro and Martina act up for the camera in Trento, Italy.

page 54

© Bill Frakes – USA
In tandem – a novel way of moving house captured on film in Miami Beach, Florida, USA.

page 55

© Luca Trovato – USA
The Gobi Desert, Mongolia – stranded with all their belongings, a nomadic family are relaxed as they await help.

pages 56–57

© Raymond Field – SOUTH AFRICA
The rhythm of the beat sets toddlers dancing to the delight of onlookers in Johannesburg, South Africa.

page 58

© Herman Krieger – USA
Surrounded by pictures of her loved ones, 92-year-old Frances reminisces on family life at her home in Oregon, USA.

page 59

© Deborah Roundtree – USA
The surprise party – a grandmother delights in the company of her grandchildren as she celebrates her 85th birthday in Yakima, Washington, USA.

page 60

© Cheryl Shoji – CANADA
In Burnaby, British Columbia, Canada, proud grandmother Dorothy soothes her first grandson as he expresses displeasure at a not-so-dry diaper.

page 61

© Quoc Tuan – VIETNAM
A grandfather and grandmother, both over the age of 70, are enchanted with their one-month-old grandson. They are playing with him on the verandah of their home in Ho Chi Minh City, Vietnam. The child was born on the couple's 50th wedding anniversary.

pages 62–63

© Sayyed Nayyer Reza – PAKISTAN
Love and kindness bridge the generation gap in Lahore, Pakistan. Nine-year-old Suman shares a playful moment with her elderly friend and neighbour – the old lady is known simply as Amman, an Urdu word for "mother".

pages 64–65

© Rachel Pfotenhauer – USA
Circles of celebration – surrounded by their family, Jean and Paul celebrate their 50th wedding anniversary at Lake Tahoe, California, USA. Reunited for this special occasion, their children and grandchildren dance in circles around the delighted couple.

page 67

© Pisit Senanunsakul – THAILAND
Two elderly friends share a joke as they go about their daily work in Chiang Rai, Thailand. They are drying native grass to be made into brooms.

page 68

© David Tak-Wai Leung – CANADA
Two Mayan children share laughter and cuddles in Panajachel, Guatemala.

page 69

© Lori Carr – USA
Body paint and childhood imagination bond young warriors Billy and Shaun in San Rafael, California, USA.

page 70

© Mikolaj Grynberg – POLAND
In Warsaw, Poland, Madame Falk's 90th birthday provides the perfect excuse for a tea party. Old friends Madame Malik, 89, and Madame Krauze, 80, share in the celebrations.

page 71

© David Williams – UK
An English tradition – deckchairs on the pier provide a typical holiday setting for three friends taking a break in Brighton, in the south of England.

pages 72–73

© John Kaplan – USA
Double happiness – as Xia Yongqing, 84, and his nephew Yang Ziyun, 82, share a joke in the village of Nanyang in the Sichuan province of China.

page 74

© K Hatt – USA
Free fall – four bikini-clad friends leap off a pier into the water below in Miami, Florida, USA.

pages 76–77

© King Tuang Wong – MALAYSIA
In Rumah Bilar in Sibu, Malaysia, young friends spend an evening making their own fun by the riverside.

pages 78–79

© Peter Gabriel – USA
A fashion-conscious trio discover the perfect accessory as they sit in a café in New York.

pages 80–81

© Kailash Soni – INDIA
Conversation comes easily to two old friends as they relax opposite the Shiv Temple of Bilawali in Dewas, India.

pages 82–83

© Guy Stubbs – SOUTH AFRICA
New faces – these young Basotho children are fascinated by 16-month-old Joshua, the first white child they have seen in their village of Bokong, Lesotho Highlands.

pages 84–85

© Janice Rubin – USA
Six-year-old dancers Natasha and Mitalee look to each other for confidence before performing in front of a capacity crowd at the Houston International Festival, Texas, USA.

pages 86–87

© Jinjun Mao – CHINA
In Shuinan village, China, the mischievous antics of a five-year-old visitor amuse and delight his grandfather and friends.

pages 88–89

© Christopher Smith – USA
Age is no barrier to enjoying a dance at a wedding party in North Carolina, USA. New bride, Pamela, teaches Uncle Mac the steps, while the bride's parents show how it should be done.

page 91

© Tino Soriano – SPAIN
Rain delays the beginning of a carnival in Barahona, Dominican Republic. A young couple exchange a flirtatious glance as they wait for the festivities to begin.

page 92

© Vincent Delbrouck – BELGIUM
Young lovers clasp each other tight as they dance to the rhythms of Havana, Cuba.

page 93

© David Sanchez Gimenez – SPAIN
A cheeky young couple distract Alfonso from his newspaper as he waits for his bus in Barcelona, Spain.

page 94

Gundula Schulze-Eldowy – GERMANY
Photographer Gundula Schulze-Eldowy can't help laughing as her friend Stephen tickles her. She set the camera on automatic to capture this self-portrait in a local park near her home in the Pankow district of Berlin, Germany.

page 95

© Tzer Luck Lau – SINGAPORE
Intimacy does not require privacy when you're a teenager living in Manhattan. These young students are absorbed in their own passionate world on a busy street in New York, USA.

pages 96–97

© Ivan Coleman – UK
London, England – two tourists share a lingering kiss by the water as the sun sets on a busy day of sightseeing.

page 99

© Renate Pfleiderer – USA
Newly wedded bliss on Long Island, New York – Travis catches Camille's wedding veil when it blows off in the wind, but he can't resist trying it on before returning it to his new wife.